The House of Elrig

This is the personal story of Gavin Maxwell's childhood and adolescence. During this time he lived mainly, either in fact or fancy, at the House of Elrig, a lonely, windswept house on the moorlands of Galloway. It is the house in which he was born and which, together with the influence of his relations, shaped his interest in living creatures and his love of wild country and wildernesses.

Besides the landscape, the birds, and his strange pets kept by him and his brothers and sister, Gavin Maxwell describes the small circle of unusual adults that formed his human horizon; the contrasting confusion and unhappiness of his early school days; the illness from which he almost died when sixteen, and the long struggle of his slow convalescence when it was only a dogged determination to return to the freedom of Elrig that sustained him. It is in the joy of that return that the book ends when the author was seventeen.

'A book to read, re-read and keep' – *Spectator*

'Will give enormous pleasure to its readers'
— *Sunday Telegraph*

D1514404

By the same author in PAN Books

RING OF BRIGHT WATER
THE ROCKS REMAIN

GAVIN MAXWELL

The House of Elrig

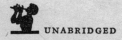

UNABRIDGED

PAN BOOKS LTD : LONDON

First published 1965 by
Longmans Green & Co. Ltd.

This edition published 1968 by
PAN BOOKS LTD.
33 Tothill Street, London, S.W.1

330 02020 ×

*This book is for The House
And all I kissed;
But greatly more than those
For children like I was,
If they exist*

Printed in Great Britain by
Richard Clay (The Chaucer Press), Ltd.,
Bungay, Suffolk

CONTENTS

ILLUSTRATIONS

(*between pages 104 and 105*)

ACKNOWLEDGEMENT

The cartoon on page 91 is reproduced from *Punch* 1925 by permission

AUTHOR'S FOREWORD

IN WRITING this story of my childhood and adolescence I have not consciously suppressed or altered anything relevant that I remember, though I have changed a few names outside the circle of my family. Although my boyhood was very unusual, I believe that some aspects find parallels in less esoteric environments, and so truth may be useful. Reading the manuscript, I became aware – which I was not while writing it – that I emerge as far from admirable. Short of deliberate falsification there is no way of improving my image. I hope that the other portraits, of those whom I loved, those whom I admired, and those who were kind to me, will be acceptable to those who felt the same, despite some irreverences. An autobiography of childhood, and an odd one at that, is bound to be subjective, and I do not claim that facts, dates, or characterizations are always accurate in an objective sense. They are what I remember. Descriptions or impressions of schools that still exist – such as Stowe – are seen through the eyes of a juvenile more than thirty-five years ago, and therefore do not necessarily correspond in any way to the present establishments.

1

THE HOUSE

YOU CAN see the house from a long way off, a gaunt, grey stone building on a hillside of heather and bracken. The road, very narrow, has climbed two or three hundred feet from the sea; slanting at first from the grey boulder beach up near-cliffs of coarse grass, bracken and thorn scrub, the few trees stunted and deformed by incessant westerly winds, so that their limbs and their heads seem to be for ever bowed and straining towards the land; on and up, winding through poor agricultural land, where the fields with their rough dry stone walls alternate with patches of scrubland, thorn bushes and briar thickets with the bare rock showing between them; through the tiny village of Elrig, with a smithy and a ruined mill but no shop; then, a mile on at the corner of a ragged fir wood sheltering a loch, is the turning to the house.

The turning is to the left, and whether you take it or whether you continue along the shore of the loch, everything for miles to that side of you is the untamed land of peat-bog and heathery hills, of sphagnum moss and myrtle and waving bog cotton, of thorn scrub and rushes and bracken; the road is the line that divides the desert from the barely sown land upon its other flank.

From the turning, the road, just wide enough to take a car, runs straight and flat across a mile of peat-bog before losing itself in the creases of the hill upon whose breast the house stands. In spring and summer the deep drainage ditches at its sides are choked with meadow-sweet and cow-parsley, and the big flat bog, 'the Moss', is sweet with the haunting trilling of curlews and the wild notes of tumbling lapwings. After a shower of rain the air smells of the bog myrtle, and big black slugs come out on to the edges of the unmetalled road. I walk

'The House of Ballingrene .. a small structure
with the sole pretension of a round tower and turret.'

The ungenteel residence — Myrton Castle

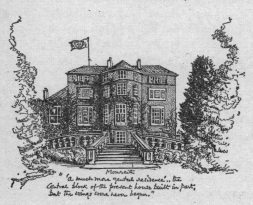

Monreith

" 'a much more genteel residence' .. the
central block of the present house built in part,
but the wings were never begun."

home at the opposite side of the road from my nurse; my mother, watching from the distant windows of the house, worries that we have quarrelled, but we are counting slugs in competition.

I was born in the House of Elrig, three months before my father was killed at Antwerp in October 1914, and only a short time after the house itself was ready for habitation. My family home, Monreith, was seven miles away on the low lands by the sea, and my grandfather who lived there was seventy when I was born, though he lived for another twenty-three years and would have gone on doing so had he wanted to.

My ancestors had been implacable expanders, and even the greatly diminished estates that he then owned (he was an implacable spender) contained the ruinous or otherwise uninhabitable remnants of two other previous seats. The first of these, the House of Ballingrene, was a small structure with the sole pretension of a round tower and turret; this Edward Maxwell was granted in 1482, and with it a quarter of the Barony of Monreith. His grandson consolidated the position in 1541 by sallying forth no less than five miles to win the hand of his cousin Margaret, who was heiress to the other three-quarters. His son, no less daring, made another sally, though of lesser distance, and married the heiress daughter of Sir Godfrey McCulloch of Myrton Castle – a much more ambitious building than Ballingrene – into which the Maxwell family then moved, and were well ensconced when William Maxwell was created a Nova Scotia baronet in 1680. Myrton Castle, on another shore of the wooded White Loch of Myrton over which Monreith now looks out, was a very beautiful but doubtless uncomfortable fifteenth-century tower. ('From the holes in those turrets,' I remember a visitor asking my grandfather, 'did they pour boiling lead?' 'Not *lead*,' he replied, and seemed at a loss to continue.)

My grandfather wrote 'My great-grandfather, having to go and attend to his parliamentary duties in London, left with his wife £2,000 to make an addition to the old castle in which

11

they lived. In what seems to us now an evil moment she listened to the advice of an architect who, as she reported to her husband in a letter still in my possession, persuaded her that he could erect on a fresh site "a much more genteel residence" than the old one. Sir William having raised no objection, the central block of the present house [of Monreith] was built in part, but the wings were never begun.' In order to build the genteel residence this vandal of an architect pulled down the greater part of Myrton Castle, leaving, by the time he had finished carting stone to the new site, little but the tower and the great walled garden; so that the glorious avenue of beeches led only to ruins and nettles.

The Maxwells, the eldest son monotonously christened William, had meanwhile avoided fame but not always notoriety, the peculiar wickedness of certain holders of the title being documented with scurrilous detail in the parish records. (The worst had a black page boy whom he beat to death, and a white horse on which he went wenching at night, wandering far afield like a tomcat and leaving not a few unacknowledged kittens.) My grandfather had been the first to achieve academic fame, though paradoxically he appears to have been the first to find his income insufficient. He inherited a sizeable estate the net rental of which, though partly moorland ground, was £16,000 per annum, and after an interminable and distinguished, though perhaps over-deployed, public career as politician (sometime Secretary of State for Scotland and a Lord of the Treasury), painter, archaeologist, historian, naturalist and writer of stupendous output, he departed this life as a Knight of the Thistle, Privy Councillor, Fellow of the Royal Society, Lord-Lieutenant of the County of Wigtownshire and Grand Old Man of Galloway; the possessor of a shrunken estate of 9,000 acres – and the noteworthy failure to have anything of any real value left in the house. (One of the few pictures of great worth was Romney's 'Jane Duchess of Gordon', daughter of the 3rd Baronet of Monreith, and her children – this he sold privately to an American visitor for £3,000. It later changed hands for more than ten times that amount.) He had, however, built on a Victorian wing to the fine eighteenth-century house, a wing which my brother later demolished, and he had formed a collection of flowering shrubs and trees among the finest in the British Isles.

For the most part these were planted flanking paths in woodlands adjoining the house; the garden itself was sloping, haphazardly planned, and surmounted by a half-circular terrace on whose gravel surface a short cut growth of box or privet spelt the Latin words of the 102nd Psalm: 'The days of man are but as grass, for he flourisheth as a flower of the field, For as soon as the wind goeth over it is gone and the place thereof shall know it no more.' Looking out over this, the glass of the old nursery window-panes on the top floor were scored by my father's initials, and I would picture him gazing down upon the rain-drenched garden and defying the words by this small act of human assertion.

There at Monreith, in a timeless feeling of money not actively spent but just disregarded, liveried footmen, and the fusty Victorian aura of dark wall paint and damp-stained bedroom ceilings, my grandfather passed his old age between his gardens and the study he had built for himself at the end of a long corridor. At the far side of this incredibly untidy room, where books were stacked everywhere on the sofas and chairs, he would sit at a big desk between two atrocious stained-glass windows, interminably writing volume after volume, answering personally all his world-wide correspondence, and contributing papers to the journals of learned societies. The rest of the big room contained a scholar's library, glass cases full of archaeological findings, and an easel bearing whatever flower painting he was engaged upon at the moment, for he had long forsaken more general subjects to record the fabulous contents of his garden.

I think he can have changed little either in habit or appearance during the twenty years or so that my memory of him covers, for my earliest images are the same as the later. He must, I suppose, have had a number of nearly identical suits, for I seem to see him in one only, of light-coloured speckled

13

Donegal tweed cut in Edwardian style, and with this he wore a high hard collar and a white silk stock decorated with a cameo pin. He stood with habitually bent knees, his body leaning back from the waist, and his chin on his chest. Throughout our childhood we called him Gar – the result, I suppose, of some babyish attempt to pronounce the word grandfather – and his unfailing annual Christmas present of £3 to each of us was known succinctly as Gar's present, spoken of for months in advance of its date in the avaricious planning of nursery and schoolroom.

He was already a widower when I was born, for following the death of his elder son in Mashonaland my grandmother's 'memory and general mental power betrayed signs of failure', to use his own words in *Evening Memories*, and by 1910 she had taken her place with the other dead of the dynasty in the lonely disused Chapel of St Medan 'to rest within sound of the

14

never-resting tide, the burial place of our family since it came to Monreith in 1481'.

His father had embraced the Irvingite creed, believing in the restoration of Twelve Apostles and the imminence of the Second Coming – (the family's disregard of financial foresight may well have been the result of this belief, and the Church demanded tithe, a tenth of the free income of all its members) – and though my grandfather apostatized in later life, his own children had been brought up in the same faith. In the British Isles there were extremely few aristocratic families who had joined the Irvingite, or, as its adherents called it, the Catholic Apostolic Church, and while there were no actual sanctions against mixed and unconverted marriages, they tended not to occur. The greatest family of the faithful was that of the Duke of Northumberland, whose parental members held themselves in more than royal state and seclusion, moving with a medieval retinue of servants between their various castles and palaces – Alnwick and Kielder, Syon, Albury and Northumberland House. Even without the bond of shared faith, my father would by virtue of his sporting and natural historic interests and his conventionally appropriate progress through Eton, Sandhurst and Grenadier Guards, have entered the peripheral orbit of this dazzling constellation. There existed, however, other strong links between the two families, for my grandfather was a boyhood friend of Northumberland, and his daughter, my aunt Christian, had married Sir John Stirling-Maxwell of Pollock, whose closest personal friend was Harry Percy, Northumberland's eldest son.

In 1909 my father married Lady Mary Percy, seventh daughter of the 5th Duke of Northumberland, one of the two beauties of the family, and brought her to Monreith. It was autumn; the trees that encroached upon the house dripped the damp grey Galloway sea fogs; even then the interior decoration of Monreith was mouldering; upstairs the feeble-minded, bedridden old lady dragged out the last year of her life in a mist of hallucination and a flicker of the nineteenth-century gas-light. It was not a happy stage upon which to set a new life.

My grandfather offered my parents the Dower house, The Airlour, a substantial but somewhat depressing building outside the west gates (here at various times of financial retreat he himself had retired, and Robert Louis Stevenson had written to him that he 'could think of nothing more romantic than living in a cottage outside your own park walls') but this did not appear to my parents to be an ideal solution to the problem of residence.

My mother was, in fact, suffering a violent reaction from the regal way in which she had been brought up. The Airlour had been built at the same period as Monreith, and could only have been appropriately restored by the reintroduction of country Adam decoration and furniture. Even such a modest compromise between grandeur and simplicity was wide of her aims; from the fabulous treasure-houses of her past homes the memories she cherished were of rugged things; heraldic, certainly, for the romance of her family's past was strong within her, but sturdy and basically functional in their far-off day. Not for her the splendours of the long gallery at Syon nor the marble hall with its gilded statues; the water-colour paintings she had brought from her former life were of massive masonry and castle walls, or a corner of the armoury at Alnwick, things of stone and of iron and of steel. She preferred the bare windswept moors of Kielder to the gentle parklands and gracious gardens of her southern homes, and the mighty bastions of Alnwick Castle against a wild sunset sky to summer lawns and deep herbaceous borders. In all her appreciation of beauty there was that which I either inherited or acquired from her, an inherent approach of melancholy or nostalgia, so that splendour could not be splendid were it not desolate too.

What she and my father wanted was a piece of land somewhere on the wilder and rougher tracts of Monreith Estate, on which to build a new house for themselves; a rugged house of the raw grey stone of grey Galloway, a house to resemble that which my uncle, John Stirling-Maxwell, had built at Corrour

16

on Loch Ossian. Rightly or wrongly, and it seems an academic question now, my grandfather refused, saying that yet another large house on the estate would only be an encumbrance, and pointing to his already advanced age as a reason for waiting for Monreith. To persist in this refusal after he knew that they were going to buy land immediately adjoining the northern-most edge of the estate can have been nothing but obstinacy, but persist he did; and this, together, I fancy, with his apostasy from the Church, set him in my mother's eyes at an angle from which he could only be seen slightly askance for ever after. Thus we saw no more of him during our childhood than the nearness of the two houses made absolutely necessary, and by the time I was growing up the abyss of age was too wide to allow more than the most superficial contact.

The flat moss road along which I walked home with my nurse counting slugs led originally to the hill sheep-farm of Aireylick. Monreith estate ended where the road stopped being straight and flat and began to climb the hill, hidden by dry stone walls. Higher up this hill was the nine-acre enclave of scrubland which my parents bought from Lord Bute, who owned the adjoining estate of Drumwalt, to build the House of Elrig. The only other entry to or exit from the enclave was a grass-grown track leading high over the moors in the direction of Drumwalt and the Mochrum Lochs. The nine acres were at a steep incline; at the lower end was a clump of elm trees holding a rookery (as a childhood sound the cawing of rooks is second only to the music of curlews and peewits), and at the higher end, with only hill and heather and sky beyond, they built the house they had planned, four-square to the winds of heaven. My mother was her own architect, and both stone and slate were quarried within a hundred yards of the site.

The house was massive, without being large by country-house standards of that generation. It was built in three storeys, crow-stepped and gabled, with one round tower, but because of the outbreak of war the top storey was never finished, never even divided into rooms. In our childhood that vast expanse of wood-lined attic was our playground, known as

The Rt. Hon. Sir

HERBERT EUSTACE MAXWELL,
Bt., F.R.S.

Politics, history, novelles
An' memories lang an' leal,
Ha'e marked him – but o'er a' things else
His Gallowa' kens him weel.

'the unfinished rooms' (cobwebs on the window-panes and sun-cracked sills, trapped Tortoiseshell butterflies beating, beating for the light, or stiff in folded-winged death, the powder spilled from the painted wings) and now, nearly fifty years later and the house sold to foreigners, they are still unfinished, still as I remember them, and there are still dead butterflies on the sills.

My mother's reaction from the past, her need for simplicity, embraced the question of furniture too; the predominant motifs at Elrig were oak, brass and pewter, and peat was the principal fuel. There was only one oil painting in the whole house, a small *pietà* of no great merit, tucked away in the decent obscurity of a corridor; for the rest there were many of my mother's water-colours, and innumerable coloured prints of Thorburn's game-birds. Halfway up the stairs hung a coloured enlargement of one of Bernard Partridge's early war cartoons, showing a blasted battlefield and a triumphant Kaiser Wilhelm addressing the King of the Belgians.

The Kaiser: 'So you see you've lost everything.'

The King of the Belgians: 'Not my soul!'

The principal pictures in the big terrace-room, which was the focal point of the house, were a large monochrome print of a flat-coat retriever at the gallop with a dead mallard drake in its jaws, and a water-colour of two wounded tigers, entitled 'Right and Left'. The floor coverings of the hall and long upstairs landing were equally rustic, though surprisingly ahead of their time, a dark red lino in big segments to resemble tiles, and rush matting that did not become a popular furnishing material for another forty years. In all the house the only piece of pretension was a big carved wooden overmantel in the terrace-room, and this too was heraldic, the Maxwell eagle surmounting a painted shield emblazoning the Maxwell and Percy arms. The matching bookcases at each side of the fire-place announced along their lintel that this was the wedding-gift of the tenantry of Monreith Estate (some of the lettering was broken by the time I first remember it, so that it read 'the gift of the TENANTRY'; this when I first learned to read I pronounced phonetically, as I did the words 'bath mat' woven into the cloth and seen from the wrong side. ('What is tamhtab?' I asked, and was deeply intrigued when I was shown the other side.)

Thought of objectively, I believe Elrig must have been one of the best-planned and most conveniently run houses I have ever seen – granted the six indoor servants (apart from nursery staff) whose presence had been implicit in its size and plan. Every room was the logical neighbour of the next, every bedroom had enormous recessed cupboard space; everything was, by the standards of the day, modern, labour-saving and bright; in sharp contrast to Monreith, where all was outdated in design and function. There, in some outhouse, an old man manufactured by some archaic alchemy gas that spurted a weak white flame from Victorian brass swinging wall-brackets; at Elrig by no lesser but more contemporary alchemy, a diesel engine converted its fuel into stored electricity. While at Monreith the woodwork was painted in sombre shades whose scatological character seemed only emphasized by faded gilt mouldings, and the walls were covered with dark Victorian tapestry, at Elrig all woodwork was of a new and experimental Gaboon mahogany, light and unpolished, and the walls were for the most part white. Monreith, lurking dankly amid its heavily wooded policies, was of the past; Elrig with its far bare horizons and arrogant defiance of the elements, seemed to challenge the future.

I was the only one of the family to be born at Elrig, and by that time my mother had already, in four years of marriage, produced three other children – first my sister Christian, and then my two brothers, Aymer and Eustace. Photographs show that during my extreme infancy we must have spent a certain amount of time at Elrig, but the greater part of the First World War, my first four years of life, we spent at one or another of my mother's maiden homes, for Elrig was too painful a place for her then. (At the age of four, enclosed within the gigantic curtain walls of Alnwick Castle, I asked my nurse

'How can we get out of this tight place?') My earliest images of Elrig, whether before or after the Armistice I do not know, are of big windswept sunny spaces, and of nursery picnics on the moor behind the house, starch-skirted nurse and nursery-maid sitting in the heather with tea-things (including table-cloth) while we threw scraps to screaming black-headed gulls that would congregate at the same time every day; the intimate security of the nursery with its peat-fire, and outside the moaning of the wind such as I have never heard in another room or house; but much stronger than these are remembered smells – bog myrtle crushed in the hand, peat-smoke, the sharp acrid tang of hill sheep and sheep-dip from the farm fank beyond the dry stone wall, the almond bitter smell and taste of caterpillar-like bracken fronds.

Although my mother was to forsake the isolation of Elrig every winter, the houses in or near London in which we would hibernate were of no importance to me, and the whole of my early childhood seems bound up with Elrig and with almost nowhere else. There was a house in London, 99 Cromwell Road, of which I remember little but a spiral staircase, the smell of the cat's cinder-box in the nursery, and the strange, almost panic, horror of seeing as we walked up Queen's Gate to the Park a presumably hysterical dog captured by the police. I was told by my nurse that it was mad, and this dog took its place in my mind beside the dead body of a cow at Elrig partially buried in quicklime because of suspected anthrax, for these two were the only threats to the all-living, all-loving mood of the nursery world I inhabited. I can place others, a little later, in their precise sequence, so sharply did each one of them shadow my sunshine; the discovery of a screaming stoat caught by the leg in a gin trap, at which I ran to my mother howling with vicarious pain and despair; the knowledge, when I was six, that not even my mother could save me from the intense pain of appendicitis; the tremendous wound to my self-respect when in the same year my sister caught me out in a lie told out of sheer cowardice.

At Elrig the day began with family prayers. After breakfast

*from a drawing by my father of himself,
my mother, and their three elder children.*

the butler would come into the terrace-room and arrange in
front of the huge oak clock-cupboard a row of nine chairs. My
mother would seat herself behind the writing-table, we four
children facing the empty row. The servants filed in, butler,
cook, housemaid, chauffeur, nurse, nursery-maid, under
housemaid, pantry-boy and kitchen-maid, and sat with their
hands folded. 'Let us pray,' said my mother, and we all
whisked round to a kneeling position. Being the youngest of
the family I had a tiny child's chair, upon which a gaudy
parrot was embroidered on a black background. The colour
and details of its plumage were connected in my mind solely
with these occasions, with my mother's voice stringing together whole rows of syllables that were quite meaningless to
me, and to which my attempts to give precise shape were a
failure. It was some years before 'the pettifullness of the great
Mersey Lucius' became intelligible as 'Let the pitifulness of
Thy great mercy loose us' and then I wondered, staring point
blank at the parrot's bill, what this was all about, because there
was nothing that I wanted to be loosed from. I was serenely

happy, and I believe that from the moment of my birth I had hardly ever cried.

I have a vivid recollection of an incident during prayers that I have been assured never took place, belonging in fact to my mother's childhood and not my own. In either case it is too splendid to omit. During my mother's concluding prayer I become aware of some sort of disturbance among the servants, and by bowing my head I am able to look under my own armpit at their kneeling behinds. The centre of the disturbance is the kitchen-maid, who has somehow managed to get her head caught between two bars of a ladder-backed chair. When the servants rise to file out she walks out chair and all with its legs in front of her like a kind of battering-ram.

There was always a governess; I can remember something of each of them in their long and usually eccentric procession, from the bosomy Madame le Roi ('don't arg, children – you must not arg'); the pathetically wispy and nervous Miss Rose with her high black buttoned boots (before she came to us she had been governess to Peter and Ian [James Bond] Fleming); the massive and masculine Irish Miss Dillan (she used to say 'Let us commence', and after her new governesses were assessed on arrival by whether or not they seemed 'commencified'); the plump and spiteful Mrs Barford with her purple woollen knitted dresses; sweet and saintly old Miss Fordham (a mealtime discussion between her and my mother on the meaning of the word 'vouchsafe' in the prayer 'vouch-safe to keep us this day without sin'; 'I think,' said Miss Fordham, 'that when I say it I mean "deign"'); and Mrs James, who looked a little like Miss Freya Stark. ('I am really Princess James, you know, but I don't use it in this country.' I don't think I ever knew what country she did use it in.)

The governesses came and went, and I never made a real friend of any of them; the only adult friend I possessed outside my family was the children's maid, Mary Gibbs, who came just before my sixth birthday and stayed for many years as a general family prop. She was not only a saint, but a human being who loved children and entered into their every activity, and she loved Elrig too. She was a warm and enduring background against which the procession of governesses filed past.

With the current governess we spent most of the morning doing lessons in what had been my father's study and was now the schoolroom; in a recess at the far side his many uniforms of Grenadier Guards, Lovat Scouts and Royal Naval Division hung in a glass case, and over the chimney-piece was a photograph of him in Grenadier uniform, surmounted by the Maxwell crest and motto, the frame carrying the epitaph of official dispatch 'his fine spirit animated his whole battalion, and it is to his example that I owe the firm and steady stand made by the Collingwoods in their trenches'.

Samples of these lessons still exist. Eustace's replies to written history questions, when he was six or seven, are rewarding.

'What do you know about Henry I?'

'Henry was a good man the people called him the good scoler because he was fond of lerning his son was drowned in the white ship. When Henry died he said that Matilder should rain but she did not because the people did not wont her to rain they wonted a man to rain so they chose Steven to be King.'

'Who was Thomas à Beckett and what do you know about him?'

'Thomas a Beckett was a preste in the time of Henry the II he was a good man. He was made Archbishop he cworeled with the King he said the prestes should be tried in a place to there selvs but Henry said they should not and Henry said who will rid me of this cworelsm peste four nites heard him and killed Thomas in the church.'

Asked to explain by illustration the words 'poverty' and 'sober', he wrote 'It is sad to see the poverty of the people in Elrig Village', and 'I am not sober because I am not quiet.' (Significantly, a set of 'laws drawn up by the three older children of Lady Mary Maxwell' – who included Eustace – contain the sentence 'Friday: Eustace allowed to come down to terrace room if quiet with a book.')

24

Armistice Day apparently did not rank as a holiday, for Christian wrote to my mother: 'We are going to do what ever lessons we like because of peace first I am going to write this letter and when we have drilling we are having flags, then we will have history then geogrurffy' – while Aymer achieved a dimmer thought 'Flags are nise and pretty and I lice them. Dogs ar to nise.' (A year or two later he wrote to one of our aunts about a snake he had seen in the garden. 'Mother hit it with a stick and crept into a hole in the wall.')

This was the era of the short story, so short, some of them, as to be positively enigmatic. 'Once upon a time there lived a bear one day the bear met a cat the cat was a wite I hope you are quite well yes thnc you said the cat good bi. THE END.' And 'Once upon a time there lived a bear in a cave. One day he met a frog I am going to kil you said the bear no don't said the frog yes I will kil you and he did THE END.'

These were Aymer's; Eustace's, too, usually ended in death or disaster, but were of more ambitious length. 'Once there lived a donkey in a field with his mrther and they were left out all night. One day they were taken in the cart but his mother had been telling him about this before and now he had found how hard it was to pull the cart and he was taking the man to the stashun *sunly* a grate eglle swopped down on the man and they got *such* a fright that he jumped up in the cart and shreeked and the donkey got *such* a fright that the donkey ran down the rode and the cart tumbled and the man was killed.' Or 'Once there lived a seagull by the sea. One day he went owt to cach fish and suddelly he sor a big shark and the shark et him up. And the shark went and told his mother she cood get seagulls to eat wenever she liked. She went and eat sikls.' Eustace's essays, however, were given to engaging asides, such as 'And did you kno when cats have kitons they pooll their tails off?'

In general they tended to lack climax, a fact emphasized by illustration – as in the following, under the title of 'Two Eagles'. 'One day two eagles were fliing acrorss the sea and they saw a big fish and the fish sed you dont no how nice it is

disgusted
the eggle were

to be down in the worter and the eagles were so disgustied that they flew away. The End.'

The windows of the schoolroom looked out on the heather and bracken of the moor, the only outdoor landscape in which I ever felt completely at home, the moor where in the afternoons we would play Red Indians, stalking a defended position.

On the moor there were two cairns of stone. The high cairn marked the rounded summit from which one could see nearly twenty miles in every direction, the Galloway hills to the east, the sea and the Mull of Galloway to the west, and to the north the long moorlands and scattered lochs of Drumwalt, blue in the purple-brown of heather. The high cairn commanded the country like a castle. The Picts had known this, and the remains of their fort lay round the cairn like a partially submerged reef, the stones lying tumbled among the heather and grown over deep with moss and lichen. The low cairn stood on a lesser eminence; one or both of these heights would be manned for our games by adults, and we children, working singly, had to take the defenders by complete surprise. As a variation, a child would be sent out as a scout or patrol from the fortress.

Where the bracken grew thick, its leaves formed a green canopy above one's head, but unless there was a wind the passage of one's crawling body through the stems produced a tell-tale ripple among the foliage. After some clumsy move-ment one would lie with heart pounding, one hand on a smooth hard bracken stem trying to steady its disturbance, the other clutching one of the slate-headed tomahawks that Hannam the gamekeeper chiselled for us with such infinite patience and skill. There were rabbits in the bracken; sometimes one came very close upon them, and the thump of a hind foot or the sudden flash of movement close at hand set one's heart ham-mering again. Turning upon one's back to rest, one looked up to see as though under a microscope the infinitely intricate pattern of bracken seeds on the undersides of the leaves, and the frothy bubbles of cuckoo-spit so close to the eye that the formation of each tiny bubble looked like a black pearl. Above the canopy of the bracken fronds flies swarmed in the sun, and the air was loud with their thin, sharp humming, metallic as their blue-black thoraxes. Slice through a bracken stem with the keen Stone Age tomahawk and one revealed in the juicy marrow the brown outline of an oak tree; the very tree, our governess assured us, in which Charles II had hidden. There were very small brown slugs about the bracken stems; these had a tendency to get between the toes (we were habitually barefoot and wore kilts of black and white shepherds plaid). The suspense of these games was as real and absolute as if they had truly been a matter of life and death, and afterwards at tea in the nursery or schoolroom there were shrill and heated post-mortems worthy in their intensity of feeling of any adult war to the death.

Being, I suppose, naturally creative children, our efforts did not stop at drawing and writing infinitely short stories; we also staged infinitely short plays. The first of these, despite pro-longed and elaborate preparation of costumes, did not, in fact get beyond the first spoken word. The play was Sir Walter Scott's *Ivanhoe*, chosen because the costumes in which Aymer and Christian had attended a children's fancy-dress party at Alnwick were appropriate, and the dialogue was taken from the novel. Aymer and Christian took the stage, part of the 'unfinished rooms', dressed as Saxon shepherd children.

Eustace, as prompter, was hidden close by, with a copy of the book open before him.

Christian addressed Aymer with confidence. 'Girth!' she said, and then was at a loss to continue. After a moment's silence she hissed 'Prompt!' and a sepulchral but very audible voice came from the hidden Eustace 'Said the jester,' he announced importantly. 'I said *prompt!*' said my sister furiously, and Eustace repeated with impatience and emphasis '*Said* the *jester.*' This dialogue continued without variation until the play broke up in disorder.

I remember others, somewhat later in our childhood, but all ending in ignominy. Conan Doyle's *The Striped Chest* for example; a singularly bloodthirsty little piece. At the moment of highest drama I got the giggles, a thing that was always liable to happen to any of us without reason or excuse. I rocked to and fro convulsed, struggling to speak my lines; then, realizing that it was hopeless, and ever ready to improvise, I gasped out 'What *has* come over me tonight?' at which the other actors became helpless too. Somehow the play survived the moment and staggered on, but my mother gave it the *coup de grâce* when she rushed on to the stage to snatch from Eustace a huge hunting-knife that, in conformity with the narrative, he was brandishing at Aymer.

Conjuring shows were popular with us but not with the servants, who, as the only available audience, were compelled to come in from their highways and their byways, until at last they went on strike and refused to attend one of mine, which wounded me deeply. Most of these shows had at least the entertainment value of the unexpected. 'I am now,' announced Eustace with falsetto pomposity, 'about to show you some of the wonders of electricity.' There was a blinding flash and all the lights in the house went out; the audience had to make their way back to their own quarters without the wonder of electricity.

Our games and our theatricals we played alone; we lived in a closed circle and met no other children. Except among ourselves we were as shy as wild animals, and the sound of unseen

28

wheels upon the steep drive sent us scuttling for cover like rabbits. To us this segregation seemed natural enough; we did not question it because we were self-sufficient. Seven miles away at Monreith among the luxuriance of tropical trees and lush blossoms the numerous children of my father's sister Winifred Graham spent much of their time, but we saw little of them until we were very much older; five miles to the north at Drumwalt Castle Lord Bute's children spent the summers,

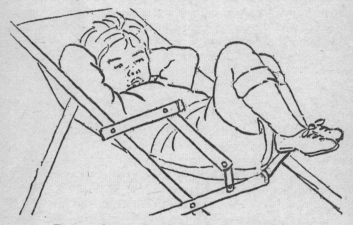

Eustace, from a drawing by Lady Muriel Percy

but our acquaintance with them did not extend beyond one courtesy visit on either side, though I remember Lady Bute riding over to see my mother, coming up over the moor track on what seemed to me to be a huge and profoundly romantic white horse. My mother had had few close friends before she married; now, apart from the obvious difficulty of keeping contact with them while burdened by four small children, I think she no longer felt their need. There were few outside visitors to Elrig; of these I remember only one clearly both because of her dazzling fire-opal jewellery and because she announced her arrival by telephone. I had not been conscious of the telephone before, and my searching inquiries elicited from my mother the explanation that it was a sort of pipe which one talked down to someone at the other end. Thereafter I called her The Pipe Lady, and spent fruitless hours trying to get in touch with her by speaking into the bath waste.

But with her own brothers and sisters my mother had always kept the closest contact, and in the world of childhood before school they were the only personalities outside her own household to make any impression upon me. They were far from ordinary people, by any standards, and two of them, together with the omnipresent ghost of my father, shaped the whole course of my youth.

2

AUNTS AND INSECTS

MY MOTHER had been one of thirteen children; of these an extraordinary number had died early in life, but during my childhood there were still six Percy aunts and uncles very actively upon the scene. Each was so marked a personality, and each was so different from any other, that to me they represented a whole cosmos of human nature. As my mother had been the only female member of her family to marry, and as all three of the surviving males had married, it was not unnaturally the three maiden aunts that played the larger parts upon our nursery stage. They had reached even further than my mother from the grandeur of their upbringing, and their tastes were simple in the extreme. Perhaps I should say two rather than three, for one of them was so wholly engrossed in her religion and the imminence of the Second Coming as to have little time for other matters.

She was Aunt Mar (Margaret), and was, I think, the eldest. When I was quite small I heard her referred to as 'a saint but mad'; both overstatements, no doubt, but even in a family of eccentrics her non-conformity was noticeable. She lived in Tedworth Square, in the days when it was peculiar for the aristocracy to inhabit Chelsea, amid a litter of china cherubims and cluttered Victoriana, and she devoted herself wholly to good works and to the Church in which she had been brought up. She was undoubtedly the plainest of the family, having inherited the Percy nose to a marked degree; she had pale marmalade-coloured hair, spectacles, and a high neighing laugh; none of these things, however, contributed as much to her apparent oddness as did her clothes, for to the very end of her life she made no concessions at all to changing fashion. I do not know at what point her sartorial consciousness had been arrested, but I should guess no later than the beginning of the First World War. Her wholly shapeless skirts, which I seem to see as fluted rather than pleated, reached to her goloshes, and her hats were of elaborate black straw. She carried a very long-handled umbrella, which I would now suspect to have dated from before the turn of the century: she used it as a walking-stick, and tapped out on the pavement her long strides. I think she found communication with children very difficult, but took great trouble about it, and like my other Percy aunts she was essentially lovable. As a small child I remember visiting her only in the company of my brother Aymer, and I remember being vividly surprised that upon opening the front door she used to address him with exaggerated and whinnying astonishment '*Why!* It's Mr *Max*!' (My brother had the same name as my father, and from his birth had been called Max so as to distinguish them.) Then she would turn to me with '*And* Mr Gavin!'

Looking back at her with the eye of middle age I see odd contradictions in the image, but of those I was unconscious at the time, accepting, as a child does, the greatest improbabilities in those who are kind and giving. It would be, for example, inside an expected general framework that she should have been out of touch, to say the least of it, with the sports of contemporary youth, and in considering what present – (she had many nephews and nieces to drain her income) – she should give me for my fourteenth birthday, ask my mother 'Has Gavin got a golfstick of his own?' – but the image becomes confused by the realization that alone among the female members of her family she used alcohol, not to excess, certainly, but as a regular feature of her meals. Her choice of alcohols was certainly not dictated by memories of her father's cellars; she habitually drank stout with her luncheon, and offered it to her unsuspecting guests as the alternative to 'a glass of wine', which turned out to be a pint of grocer's port. I do not remember ever seeing her away from her own home, except at church; I suspect that her human horizons, like her interests, were wholly limited by circumstance to the members of her faith, a faith that as a child I shared without question or curiosity, sitting wearily through the age-long sermons and services held by tottering old men who had no power to ordain successors. Just as the first twelve apostles had believed that Christ would return during their lifetimes, so eighteen hundred years later those who believed themselves called as a second twelve did not doubt it either. Only they and none other had the power to ordain new ministers (a real proof of this Church's absolute integrity) – and by the time I was born the last of them had been long dead. Hope there must have been, to hold those dogged congregations together even after, many years later, almost all of the ministers had died and the churches stood for the most part empty, but hope was not in those days evident to a child; the tired trembling old voices – voices belonging, each one, to personalities of patently unusual saintliness – that read the prayers seemed to be reciting dirges of dreary defeat, and the adult choirs sang at a tempo so slow that all music seemed to be lament. The churches of our faith were to me from the beginning places of infinite depression and sadness, epitomized by the memory of Good Friday services and a voice born of some bottomless despair giving back the reiterated response to a litany: 'For thou hast crucified thy Saviour.' During the silence of the Communion, various members of the priesthood or of the congregation would pass into a trance-like state and begin to prophesy in a loud voice that was terrifying to my childish ears. Sometimes they spoke in English, or whatever their native tongue was, and sometimes in no known language; of words intelligible to me I can remember only an old man with staring eyes looking towards the altar and enunciating 'Comfort ye, comfort ye, my people, for your Lord cometh,' and once 'I am the God of Gods, saith the Lord; I am the Lord of Hosts; I am the God of Abraham and of Isaac. Open your eyes that ye may see.' This 'speaking in the spirit', as it was called, was as awe-inspiring and frightening to me as would have been the distorted voice of the Sibyl fused with escaping gases from the turbulent mountain, at the Delphic omphalos. As if emerging from a family death-bed scene, it would be half an hour or more after one was out of church that it seemed to me decent to talk of ordinary mundane matters; into this fathomless bath of guilt and grief we returned for a weekly dip of four hours every Sunday that we spent in England. One of the aims of our Church was that it should not be sectarian, and so its members were encouraged when out of reach of its own services to attend those of any other Church; thus when we were at Elrig we went to the Church of Scotland at Mochrum, where not only were the services of a very different kind but also my mother tolerated a certain amount of levity in subsequent mimicry of the minister's voice and mannerisms – levity that would have been unthinkable towards the hierarchy of our own Church. The Kirk of Mochrum, with its single bell hand-tolled by rope by a black-clad blacksmith standing among the spring crocuses and daffodil clumps outside, enshrined a treasure-house for our mimicry. We sat upstairs, in a gallery pew with an excluding gate (here in earlier times the Maxwells had relaxed in armchairs with a private fireplace and rattled the poker when the length of a sermon became intolerable) looking down upon the little harmonium, the choir of local worthies grouped round it, and the wooden pulpit from which the black-robed minister conducted the whole service in a high, sonorous and artificial voice. Random from a thousand recollections of those services, attended to almost with avidity for the sake of subsequent parody, are: 'Let us worrrship God, to His praise let us sing hymn number one nothing nothing.' 'So when the collection plate comes round just put a sixpence in it for the sake of Jesus Christ – *and your own repute*!' 'So, my brethren when you are given the new hymn books don't leave the old lying about in the pews – I've seen that happen once in a given case, and a very unseemly thing it was in the Kirk of Christ – just consign them to God's clean flames.' There were two sermons, one for children ('So, children just remember there's Bethany and Bethlehem, *and don't get them mixed up*!') and another, a full hour long, for the adults, consisting for the most part of infinite repetition of

34

the same phrase with varying intonation to disguise the vacuity of thought.

The only beauty of the family besides my mother had been Aunt Tor (Victoria), and she preserved until her death in old age an extraordinary sweetness of expression. Photographs of her as a girl show a face of such loveliness that she cannot possibly have lacked for suitors, but she too remained a spinster, and during our childhood often shared houses in England with my mother. She was not often at Elrig; her slight unassuming form and primmed-back hair concealed a personality of such enormous drive and energy that she could seldom spare time to be away from whatever her business was at the moment – public works, high-pressure chicken farming or (the last of her enterprises) the largest fur rabbit farm in the world. During the First World War she had occupied the position of Commandant of the Red Cross Hospital at Alnwick, and after the Armistice she had brought to live with her as companion a retired Nursing Sister named Miss Sadler, also of the faith. Miss Sadler had sustained an injury to one leg, and walked with a heavy rubber-tipped stick. I never liked her; whether because she knew how to use a sharp tongue on a child, or because in the tiny enclosed group of our family I felt her to be an intruder, she irritated me as no doubt we irritated her. At her most good-humoured she had a kind of heartiness which I felt to be out of key, epitomized by her description of Dürer's drawing as 'those jolly praying hands'.

I have never known why Aunt Victoria did not marry. She would have made a wonderful wife and a wonderful mother; in all the years I knew her I never heard her speak an unkind or ungracious word, and I felt for her a deep and unmixed affection.

While Aunt Victoria was a steady background to a large part of every year, one of the landmarks of security, she was not a formative influence except in so far as her firm gentleness asked emulation. By contrast, the youngest of the sisters, Aunt Moo (Muriel) was a tremendous stimulus. She loved

35

children, would take infinite trouble over them, and possessed in high degree the power to arouse and hold their interest in new things. Like the rest of her family she was extremely unconventional. Slightly mannish, noticeably square-shouldered and with a masculine walk. Fair hair and a bun, large pale blue eyes with a slight cast, and a deep drawling voice that afforded us endless opportunity for imitation. She had two long hairs on the centre of her chin; when asked why she did not have them removed she replied coyly 'I like to play with them.' She habitually wore a well-cut coat and skirt of grey flannel and a white silk shirt. Unlike Aunt Victoria she was prone to salutary outbursts of irritation and forthrightness, but her drawl was so pronounced that her customary explosion of 'Oh for *heaven's* sake!' took at least twice the normal time to get out. Many years later I met her at the funeral of an elder aunt, and mumbled something silly and consolatory. She fixed me with an abstracted squint for a long moment before replying 'I caan't understairnd why you say thairt – she's faar betta where she is.' She was a serious research zoologist with a preferred interest in the inhabitants of pond and rock pool (her own special study had been the parasites upon the water-flea) and one of her most imitated dicta became 'Put it bairk, Mairx – it's a water shrimp and it does not like to be on the lairnd.' (The remark was actually made to my cousin Hughie, but the name did not lend itself to the same distortion.) Outside these specializations, however, she was an exceedingly good general naturalist – nothing that flew, crawled, crept or ran escaped her inquiring eye and mind, and her enthusiasm for uncovering the secret lives of these lesser creatures, most especially the insect world, communicated itself to us like mercury filling an empty tube.

She painted in water-colours and drew in line – not land-scapes nor inanimate objects but illustrations of the creatures that interested her and she hoped would interest us; and to me, anyway, she brought a fairyland into the nursery. I remember her assembling upon the table my first glimpse of it – a painted background that stood up like a stage backcloth, and in the foreground painted cardboard cut-outs of bright fungi, butterflies and caterpillars, each one labelled with its name. I can also remember seeing in her own face the reflection of the pleasure she gave me.

Thereafter our journeys to the sea-shore below the lonely Chapel of St Medan became voyages of discovery. It was always sunshine. We would set off in the only car my mother possessed, a 1914 Ford with brass lamps and radiator – (heated derision of my sister when she claimed to have been driven at a full 30 mph along the shore road) – a chauffeur at

the wheel, my mother wearing a mauve motoring-veil. We children sat in a row on the folded-down hood, our feet dangling above the back seat, singing and shouting and chattering with anticipation. When we came in sight of the sea from the top of the grass cliffs (called 'heughs' in Galloway, and practically unpronounceable) it looked sparkling like imperfectly smoothed silver-paper; we had our own word for this – 'shinkly' and the shinkliness added to our exhilaration because it added even more light and movement to the sky and the salt wind in our faces.

Below the old chapel, low on a heugh where the wind had styled the treetops to the contour of the land like hair combed back from a forehead, there was a long stretch of hard sand at low tide, and on the point beyond the solitary lobster-fisher-man's hut there were boulders and an infinity of sea pools. Beyond that again were black rock cliffs with deep mysterious caves full of the whicker of rock-pigeon's wings, and ravens wheeling overhead. My mother would gather buckets of lim-pets and periwinkles, while we pottered and paddled and my aunt discovered for us ever-fresh wonders by the edge of the tide. From these expeditions we brought back in bottles curious and fascinating creatures of the rock pools, sea-anemones, sea-slugs and such like; these my aunt would paint with a deftness that seemed to me miraculous, and as she painted she discoursed upon their lives and 'hairbits', so that much of those baby lessons remain with me to this day.

But the sea was several miles away, and we could not go there every day; my aunt was quick to show us that things as marvellous inhabited every yard of the garden and the moor-land. There was a tiny water garden rich with purple flag iris, and among them a pool known as 'Daddy's Pool' (it was approached through a dense hawthorn thicket in which my mother had carved a tunnel and a deep bower known to us as Mother's Den); here we learnt the slimy mysteries of frog-spawn and tadpoles, newts and aquatic insects such as the big rowing beetle and the Giant Water Boatman (spelled by brother Eustace, in his conscientious account of it, as the Gyant Woter Botman). From a rock in the centre of the pool, which cannot have been much more than four yards across, we would watch for hours the movements of these creatures. With the child's ephemeral power of confining all thought and per-ception to the horizons of the moment, that world beneath the surface – a surface reflecting the swordleaves and purple flowers of the irises and the cumulus clouds and our own faces – became at these times the only world outside myself, the actions of its inmates the only significant thing. Returned to the nursery and our toys, or to my constant and laborious embellishment of my Book of Birds and Animals – an illus-trated and highly imaginative opus which I was dedicating to my mother – these worlds, too, would be as complete in themselves, as impossible of extension.

The Book of Birds and Animals was the precursor, more general in scope and less lavishly decorated, to the Book of Birds with Beautiful Tails, an illustrated monograph in the great tradition of the genre. Meanwhile I illustrated Birds and Animals and dictated the text to my sister, for none other than I could be trusted to unscramble the strange mysteries of these creatures' lives.

'*The Crested Bird*. This is a foreign bird you find his eggs in foreign lands they would be about as big as the biggest persons head if you compaired the sizes. The bird in the picture is a cock bird he is called the Crested bird because of his great crest. The next picture is of the hen bird of this sort.

'*The Green Bird*. This bird lay 100 eggs in a year. They are brownish white. He has eggs of an eggish shape.

'*The Blue Headed Bird*. The nest of the blue Headed bird is made of moss and sticks and grass and bracken the eggs are white speckled with black. The hen bird of this sort is very suitable for her husband.

'*The Skiping Long Nose*. He lives in America like the Mustangs. He has babies almost as big as their mothers. The mothers are only as big as your head, and the babies only as big as that little bit of cardboard on the windowsill.

'*The Brown Legged Hinda*. Does eat chalks and knifes and blue eyes and grass his babies are brown and white.

'*The Ruvvled Bird*. You can see in the picture I was rather careless about for she was not in the mood for it. He has got blue eggs specled with pink she is a very horrid bird.

'*The Blue Crested Bird*. This bird lays 12 eggs of white specled with black, it lays its eggs in various places though they are curious places too. She has red brown eyes the colour people admire.

'*The Nicest Bird*. She lays eggs bluish black, she lives in forests in Africa. She makes her nest strange to say in wild african's houses.

> 'Dear Mother
> 'from Gavin
> 'The End. Christmas 1919.'

Even when we were away from Elrig, wintering drearily in England, I would send to Aunt Moo finds for identification and comment. Not long ago, searching the attics of Monreith for relics of those early days, I came across a small cardboard box addressed in her handwriting to Master Gavin Maxwell, and with a legible postmark of 1921. It contained a fossil sea-urchin that I had sent to her from my winter exile at Harrow-on-the-Weald, and a letter from her describing what the object was. I reproduce the letter in full, as a perfect example of how a child's interest can be aroused and held.

'This is the shell of a Sea-Urchin called Cidaris, which lived probably about 8,000,000 years ago. There are some very like it alive now, but they live at the bottom of the sea, so we don't often meet them.

'They have club-headed spines, instead of long prickly ones like other Sea-Urchins.

' "Urchin" is a name for a hedgehog – so Sea-Urchin means Sea Hedgehog, – because of its prickliness. Harrow Weald was once the bottom of a deep, still sea and white chalk formed very thick on this sea-floor, from the remains of sea beasts and shells. The shells of Sea-Urchins sank into this white soft stuff, when the urchins died, and hard lumps of flint often formed round them, because the salts and minerals in the chalk and in the water joined together to make flint, so that rain and the frost broke up the soft white chalk, and wore a lot of it away, and then people came and used it for making bricks with. So the chalk is all gone at Harrow, but the hard flints are left, and in them the prints left by the shells and spines of the old urchins. Now the shell or "test" as it's called is made up of separate armour-plates, and in Cidaris each plate grew one *large* club-headed

40

spine, from the bump in the centre – as well as lots of *little* club-spines all round on much smaller bumps.

'The spines were fixed like one's own shoulder on a ball and socket joint, with muscles attached so that the urchin could wave them about, and run on them when it was hurried. They were very, very hard, and pricked the beasts who tried to eat the urchin. The urchin lived inside the shell, but his skin oozed out, – jelly-fashion, – between the plates of his armour, and spread in a thin film all over the shell, so that he could attend to the muscles of his spines, and pull them about in all directions.

'Besides all this, you see five twisting bands running round the shell; these are covered with rows of tiny holes, for his little feet to come through; he had dozens of little sucker feet, that he pushed in and out of his shell, and walked with in any direction – upwards or downwards, or sideways; backwards or forwards, among the rocks and stones.

'When I broke your big flints, further, I found two prints of urchin plates still joined together. You might find lots more, just by turning over stones, without breaking. There were many different kinds of Cidaris, with variously-shaped spines.'

My father's gun-room, unused since his death, became, under my aunt's organization, a sort of primary school for the study of life. There were aquaria full of hatching frogspawn or tadpoles in metamorphosis; newts in hibernation; Gyant Woter Botman sculling the periphery of new quarters; the spider-like Water Measures scurrying across the meniscus of the water, measuring things at incredible speed; vivaria in which caterpillars munched leaves like locusts or pupated into strange but beautiful chrysalises (the incredible, intimate touch of the child finger upon the chrysalis of a new pupated moth caterpillar, the almost horrifying wriggle from life not yet dormant inside the horny casing); a glass-fronted cage in which huge woolly-bear caterpillars grazed upon sweet-smelling bunches of heather; the sections of heavily tunnelled rotten wood inside which the great white grubs of the Giant Syrex were awaiting transformation into a huge hornet-like insect; the bright, jewelled bodies of solitary wasps and leaf-cutter bees – these and many others my aunt laid before us as our patrimony, so that whenever we stepped beyond the doors of the house we were on nodding terms with almost every living thing we could see. We knew their names and something about their 'hairbits'; 'one of the nicest things about us,' she said to me, 'is that we are interested in them while they're not interested in us.'

We began to specialize, each of us, very early, though our specialization had probably as much to do with the structure of our family unit as with any personal preference. Each of us referred to the remainder of the group as 'the others' (also addressed in the vocative case as 'Others!') but the image of the others must in each case have been sharply individual. My sister, I think, identified herself with none of us, and never found the deep preoccupation with lesser lives that her brothers did. She must of necessity have been lonely in a childhood that contained none of her sex and age. She probably tried to dominate me, but a child does not formulate these ideas and so I was unconscious of it. Facially and mentally she was a product of our breeding, the same stock as Aymer and myself, but Eustace was the odd man out, a throwback. He was extrovert, bouncy, aggressive, self-sufficient, of explosive temper very easily repaired, and I remember discovering with a profound shock that he could flout the gods of authority. When very small he would, after any difference of opinion with my mother, take a firmly retaliatory stand, remaining coldly aloof, and resisting all attempts at verbal cajolery by the haughty words 'Not noticing Mother.' The only physical punishment that my mother used – very rarely and under intense provocation – was to slap us; my invariable reaction to this was to burst into tears, not because of the pain but because of the reproof, and to me it was unthinkable not to. The first time that I remember seeing Eustace slapped he not only did

42

not burst into tears but he just stood giving my mother back look for look. I felt as if a thunderbolt must strike him or the earth swallow him up for this dreadful blasphemy, so I cried instead. My sister asked me what I was crying about and I couldn't possibly explain.

Eustace began immediately to specialize in bees and wasps – the many different kinds of bumble-bee, and the gem-like solitary bees and wasps. He collected them both alive and dead, the wings and limbs of the latter arranged with infinite care and patience on the same kind of setting-board as is used for butterflies. The collecting was rather like Happy Families – a set of each species of bumble-bee had to include a queen, a drone and a worker. He took wild hives and fed them on sugary concoctions (bottles labelled OWNITE FOR BEES contained no greater magic than a mixture of brown and white sugar) and got himself stung with mechanical regularity. (It was, I think, a good deal before the bee days that he ran howling to my mother about a terrible pain in his ear that, he blubbered, was due to a large green beetle inside it. This diagnosis was not unnaturally treated as fanciful. However, at the second drop of soothing ear lotion out walked a large green beetle.)

Eustace collected every kind of insect but beetles, specializing particularly in bees and wasps. Aymer collected beetles. I collected butterflies, dragon-flies (I caught very few) and birds' eggs. But while Eustace's collection was a strictly individual enterprise, I was always obsessed with a desire for partnership. 'Will you share . . .?' was the opening gambit for merger, and 'Will you share my collection of eggs?' led to a long partnership with my eldest brother that lasted right through our childhood and adolescence. My efforts to share my collection of butterflies were constant but met with no permanent reward; I shared it with Aymer for a short time, very briefly with Eustace, and finally, in desperation, with my sister. But I succeeded in sharing Aymer's collection of beetles, for in me he had a willing servant to do all the really disgusting jobs that this particular collection involved. I know that small, beautiful and inoffensive beetles do exist, and I suppose that some of them must have featured on Aymer's lists, but all that I remember were creatures of peculiar horror. We would set off, he and I, on a beetle hunt, up one of the grassy tracks over the moor, I carrying the weapons of the hunt; a 'killing bottle' with a broad cork and ammonia-soaked cotton-wool at the bottom, a collecting-box in which to carry the nauseating carcases and a handkerchief with which to effect capture. Beetles, apart from huge rotund blue-black dung beetles that might be encountered struggling ponderously along with a ball of dung almost anywhere, lived under things. When the things were stones it wasn't so bad. Aymer heaved over the stone while I stood ready with the handkerchief to seize whatever was scurrying for safety among the worm tunnels and white grass roots. Centipedes and millipedes we ignored – beetles were our business. The commonest (I can see them now, scuttling for the grass or dead bracken at the edge of their ruined homes) were about an inch long, black on top and red underneath, with thin red legs. Devil Coachhorse beetles, thin and black, holding their tails over their backs like scorpions, were worthy of capture; I think there were several sorts, one rare. We would move on. The next object to be turned over would be something highly prized by my brother – the carcase of a dead animal, a rabbit or a hare. Dead for some time; eyes gone from the sockets, fur flattened and hard like cement; anyone without my experience would have said that this was a withered, dried-up thing, past smelling. But lifting it gingerly by an ear a whole world of horror lay revealed beneath. The juices of the body had oozed into the ground, leaving a sort of yellowish pus that stank worse than any other carrion that I have ever smelled – possibly because my nose has never been quite as close to it since. A whole kingdom of frightful creatures inhabited this sickening slime – thin white whip-like worms, fat wriggling bluebottle grubs – and carrion-eating Burying Beetles. Slow-movers, surfeited by their nauseous feast, legs groping to escape the unaccustomed light. Small heads and big square red-and-black striped bodies. Holding my nose with

44

one hand, it was my job to pick these up with the handkerchief and drop them into the killing bottle held open by my brother, where the armoured legs waving slowly in death agony completed a revolting tableau.

These things I did without question, because I worshipped my brother – not, I think, as a hero in those days, but as some extension of myself. We, the eldest and the youngest brothers, became like twins; I was not actively happy without him, and I think he was not actively happy without me. This relationship, somehow separating us from the rest of the family, began to form when I was about six and he was about eight. It meant that in a family of four children the other two had to pair off or remain solitary, and my sister Christian and brother Eustace were so different that they couldn't pair. Only when my brothers went to school, and I was left at home sharing a governess with my sister four years older, did we form as much of a partnership as the difference in age and sex allowed. It was then that, very temporarily, I tried to 'share' my collection of butterflies with her; it didn't work because she wasn't interested and for the first time I found myself quite alone in my pursuits. I found them curiously enhanced, because I had never had a private 'unshared' world before. At the age of six or seven I would go off quite alone with my butterfly-net and killing bottle, alone among the bog myrtle and heather under the windy summer sky and I would swipe and miss and cry because I'd missed, and I learned what it was to be alone. Having learned it, I wanted no other day-long company than my own, excepting my brother Aymer's, and this remained true for years.

For my age I suppose I knew a lot about butterflies and moths. I knew and had collected all the species that were common at Elrig, and from the picture-books in which I would get lost in reverie I knew what all the other British butterflies looked like, even to the magic Camberwell Beauty – somehow equated in my mind with my only sight of the Crown Jewels at the Tower of London, an unbelievable splendour flowering from crimson velvet. Far into my adult life I retained a

45

curious, quite precise feeling of exhilaration and wonder at seeing for the first time in the flesh some bird or beast that before I had known only from pictures, as if one were meeting for the first time some notoriety long worshipped from afar. I can remember one of these occasions with an extraordinary subjective vividness, besides experiencing the scene as a tableau viewed from outside as though I were a spectator of somebody else's action. A little boy of about five or six, dressed in a black-and-white check kilt, a grey flannel shirt, a white cotton sun-hat. He is carrying a butterfly-net and killing bottle, and he stands in a marshy hollow filled with bog myrtle and rushes. Suddenly a very large butterfly whizzes past at very high speed, but not so fast that the boy cannot recognize it as something he has never seen, but whose coloured portraits he has pored over in illustrated butterfly books. The butterfly passes but does not disappear, it goes on racing round, always out of range of the swiping net. The boy falls to his knees – prickles of myrtle stems among the soft sphagnum moss – and starts praying aloud. 'Please God let me catch the Dark Green Fritillary.' And God answered my prayer, strengthening an absolute belief that could not be called into question.

I can see them all in their glory; the splendid burnish on the wings of a Small Copper as he fans them gently, poised on the round blue cushion of a scabious flower; the satin sheen, so delicately bordered with seed pearls, of a Common Blue, or folded upward to show the wings' underside, the pearls arranged as an even layer on a surface of white kid; the peach and pale velvet of a Painted Lady; the aggressive tiger colouring of the Tortoiseshells on the sun-cracked sills of the long attic; the hard, burning shimmer of the little hunting wasps, each as bright as a cut jewel. I saw them all in their glory with the undimmed and finely focused eye of a six-year-old, and though their descendants are resplendent still they can never be quite so bright as those seeming heralds of the millennium.

3

ENTRANCE OF A HERO

AFTER MY Aunt Muriel the next member of my mother's family to make lasting impact upon me was the awe-inspiring figure of my Uncle William Percy. For him I conceived a profound and lasting admiration, perhaps making him in childhood a substitute for the father whom I lacked. His face was familiar to me from the very earliest days I can remember, long before he first came to Elrig, for a framed photograph of him hung on the wall of my mother's bedroom, a studio portrait in which a barrister's wig topped a face that was handsome, aquiline and arrogant, looking down into the camera's lens with a sort of impatient mockery. Uncle Willie was the perfect Buchan hero, not a Hannay, for he was too taut and fine drawn for that, nearer to Sandy Clanroyden, but with a far harder streak of steel in him and none of that 'Dick old man, I'm most awfully pleased to see you'.

Though he had been in turn explorer, barrister, soldier, secret agent and Deputy-Governor of Jerusalem, his one enduring love from his boyhood until his death was natural history, and ornithology in particular. No passive or distant love, this; a passionate spirit of inquiry and a desire to uncover what he would call with great emphasis *fact* animated his whole life with restless energy; he was about the birds' beds and their baths and spying out all their ways. Thus he made some remarkable contributions to knowledge, discovering, for example, why a heron has a powder-puff in the middle of his back (to clean eel slime from its beak). He was an advocate of pure science; to anyone who did not share his interests and questioned the value of such discoveries he would merely reply, 'There is a book who runs may read.'

He must have been in his mid-thirties when I first remember him, and I remember my mother explaining that he was sometimes irritable or bad-tempered because he had been so terribly wounded in the war that his shoulders were held together by wire and he was often in pain. He was short and slim and wiry, and dressed habitually in riding-breeches and a belted Norfolk jacket. Everything about him was crisp and incisive, his voice, his gestures (I remember how he would take a cigarette and tap each end of it twice upon his case with a brisk, almost triumphant movement, as though he were giving the *coup de grâce* to some impudent enemy), his short springy hair parted in the middle. One was conscious of the pupils of his brilliant eyes in the same way that one is conscious of the muzzle of a gun pointed straight at one; his glance was impossible to ignore.

I was fascinated by him, a little as a rabbit is fascinated by the antics of a stoat; everything about him had the panache of pyrotechnics.

I must have been quite small when I first heard my mother say to another grown-up that Uncle Willie knew no other form of conversation than that of cross-examination, and that even then the cross-examined was bewildered to find that in the course of the first minute he had been transferred from the witness-box to the dock. The voice *attacked*, the lips pressed tightly against the teeth, projecting from the extreme front of the mouth a slow machine-gun fire of words, almost all of which were separately and individually italicized. Only very rarely could a victim stand up to the simultaneous fire of the eyes and voice; the few who did were astonished to find themselves suddenly attacked from the rear, for Uncle Willie held to the military maxim that a weak position should never be reinforced, and was always ready to change the whole standpoint of his argument if any return missile landed dangerously near. To him this was a game, far more stimulating than chess, which he also loved, and the break-up of his opponent into temper or tears caused him infinite and obvious glee. His method of bridgehead into enemy territory was usually to exploit the comparatively loose way in which most laymen confuse proven fact with belief or supposition. Alerted by years of practice to detect the least weakness in factual knowledge, the first tacit admission of ignorance would swing the big guns into action:

'Well, it's no use arguing if you *don't know your facts*!'

I only heard one person avoid this bludgeoning, and that was his wife, my Aunt Polly, who had all the complementary virtues, so that to stay at their home was to encounter a wholeness that one sees seldom in a lifetime. She, quite unruffled, would reply, 'Surely you know me well enough by now to know that I've got no *exact* knowledge about anything.'

Sometimes, when there was patently some truth in his opponent's view, or when he himself was arguing from ignorance (and this was not seldom) he proceeded more warily:

'Do you really believe that? You do?'

This left the field open. Or:

'If that's true, it's extraordinarily interesting.'

A doubt remained in his opponent's mind, and that was enough. Sometimes his strategy dictated an apparent surrender:

'Of course you're *absolutely right*, right down the line!' Then, before the other could register a victory, 'And what are you going to do about it?'

To establish the full flavour of his personality I must jump the nursery years into adolescence and early manhood, for as small children we were unworthy of his rapier wits. It was a dozen years later, for example, that I arrived to stay at his farm on the Norfolk Broads, and I had hardly been in the house ten minutes when he drew me to the chimney-piece of the sitting-room. Picking up a curious, curved piece of bone perhaps a foot long, he put it into my hand with the words,

'What's *that*, Gavin?'

I turned it over and tried to use my brain on it while he looked at me expectantly with a thin, pre-triumphant smile. At length I hazarded that it appeared, if it was in its original state, to be a bone that had not been articulated, a floating bone. He looked very slightly disconcerted, so I knew I was on the right track, but he just said '*Well?*' I tried to think of floating bones, and the only thing of that size I could think of was the vestigial thigh bone of a whale. I said so. '*Wrong! Gavin, wrong!*' he exclaimed delightedly, 'Well, *well!* You ought to have known *that* one, oughtn't you! It's the *penis bone of a walrus!*'

There were other objects on the chimney-piece. Uncle Willie had just returned from a South American gold-mine in which he had an interest, and there were two lumps of yellowish ore. He handed them to me and said 'What are *those*?' I fell straight into the trap and I said they looked like gold. '*Wrong again!* Of *course* they look like gold, but they're *not*. You wouldn't make much of a gold-miner, *would* you?'

Later in the evening we discussed the possibility of his giving me a holiday job as farm-hand. 'Well,' he said, 'I certainly couldn't afford to pay you the wages of an ordinary farm labourer! You wouldn't describe yourself as a very husky specimen, would you?'

Also to adult life belonged an occasion when I met him in my mother's house in London in the late morning and said, 'I suppose you won't lunch with me, will you, Uncle Willie?' The reply was immediate and emphatic. 'No I *won't*, Gavin, no I *won't!*' Similarly, one would tell him some long and exciting story or theory, all under the bright mocking stare, and the only response at the end would be 'Do you believe that?' or sometimes 'Well, if you believe that you'll believe anything'. (As a crusher, I have only heard one better comment at the end of a story narrated at length. I knew a Highland stalker, who at the conclusion of some epic tale recounted with feeling and excitement, would mutter 'So I suppose, major, so I suppose'.)

Similarly, my uncle would listen to an enthusiastic, artless and lengthy description of a bird that some guest in his house had seen, and when the final question came 'Now, what bird was that, Lord William?' he would answer coldly 'There is no such bird' and, if possible, exit on this line.

But for pure verbal economy in attack a telephone conversation with my brother Aymer remained unchallenged. 'Well,' my uncle had said briskly, 'you wanted to see me. What time do you propose?'

'Any time you like, Uncle Willie; I'm free all day.'

'*Free all day!* Wheeeeeew!' The whistle was prolonged over several seconds.

Once he appeared at a shooting-party at Monreith, dressed in singular and handsome soft white leather gaiters and combined spats. Another guest, a contemporary of ours, approached him diffidently and said:

'Forgive my asking, Lord William, but where did you get those wonderful gaiters?' Uncle Willie eyed the speaker for a second before assessing him as the right material for a quick verbal snack. '*Get* them?' he said testily; 'You can get them anywhere, as far as I know. I happened to get these in Pernambuco, as a matter of fact.' Later in the day, when the party was crossing a field on which small piles of lime were waiting to be spread, my uncle hurried up to the same young man, pointed to the lime and asked with great vigour 'Buchanan – *what is that?*' Slightly disconcerted by the intensity of the question, Buchanan replied 'It looks to me like lime, isn't it?' My uncle, for once unexpectedly baffled by an accurate reply to his fire, said 'Lime? Of *course* it's lime, Buchanan; of *course* it's lime!'

He was a close friend of Colonel Dick Meinertzhagen whose exploits in Kenya were famous; he was a legendary figure to me, made even more ogre-like by Uncle Willie's reply to some particularly inane remark of mine. 'Gavin – Dick Meinertzhagen's coming to stay next week. I wouldn't say things like that in front of him if I was you – *he's killed men with his bare hands!*'

When I first remember Uncle Willie nearly half of his spectacular life lay behind him, and perhaps less than half of his travels, that embraced ultimately the greater part of the earth's surface. Recalling some far-off journey, conjuring with great and lightning vividness some happening distant in time and place, he would conclude (without a sigh): 'It's nice to have done these things; I don't know that I want to do them again.' I think that when he became my childhood hero his remote travels had been mainly to the Canadian and Siberian Arctic and to the interior of Africa. At the beginning of the Second World War I arrived home from East Finnmark just in time, and in response to a telegram, to avoid being trapped in Scandinavia; my uncle's comment was: 'Well, you were in a much easier position than I was at the beginning of the First World War, *weren't you*? I was *five hundred miles north of the Bering Straits*, carrying the most important collection of arctic duck skins ever made!' In fact this was no exaggeration, and ever since many a museum in many a country has relied for knowledge upon the fruit of his enthusiasm, knowledge and extraordinary manual skill. (He was also, incidentally, one of the very finest shots who ever lived.) Later, he travelled practically the whole of the American continents and much of the Middle East.

The force of his personality made him utterly independent of class distinctions; he was far indeed from a dilettante scion of a noble house. He was immensely tough, immensely self-sufficient, and very very clever. If he had been born statusless he would have risen by sheer quality to control whatever he wanted to control. He despised people who employed others to do jobs they had time to do themselves (blistering comments on my employing a local garage to repair a car's punctured tyre when I was nineteen) and detested inefficiency in any walk of life; and seemingly because of his enormous energy he carried with him a magnetism that affected animals as well as humans. The following passage is quoted from an American obituary notice by Robert Cushman Murphy.

'Without meaning to be mystical, I am convinced that some subtlety of Lord William's approach proved as winning to animals as to his fellow men. I recall an occasion at his former farm near Great Yarmouth when a huge sow with eight or ten farrow repulsed the pig-keeper at every attempt to enter the sty and pick up a suckling which had lacerated jowls. Lord

William, on his rounds, asked the man to try once again. When this produced another infuriated response, his Lordship vaulted the fence himself, pulled the baby pig by its ear from the teat of a wholly complacent mother, and carried it off for medication.'

In the same obituary are quoted Uncle Willie's own words which splendidly defined his own position.

'Man, the arch-destroyer and predator in all creation, whose history is degraded and disgraced in every generation by its record of ruthless destruction and brutality inflicted in greed or lust on the animal creation and on his fellow man alike, is wont to describe the law of Nature in such hackneyed and unthinking phrases as "red in tooth and claw", and yet may search the operation of that law in vain for similar perpetration of cruelty by wild creatures.'

Towards the end of his life he returned from one of his African expeditions with a fever so critical that he had to be rushed ashore before his ship docked. A few weeks later I collected him from a London hospital to take him to the Norfolk train. For the first time in all my remembrance of him he looked an old man; the glitter had gone from his eyes, and his speech and movements had become slow. (This phase did not last.) On the drive to the station, I asked him some question about elephants in the Congo, from which he had returned, but he did not answer it. He stared out of the window at the wet streets and the press of London traffic, and after a very long pause he said, as if to himself, 'They're no good, you know. Their ivory's all soft.' Had this remark been made during our childhood we should undoubtedly have adopted it as a synonym for what he despised and detested – inefficiency of any sort. His own ivory hardened again, and remained hard until the day he died exactly as he would have wished, absolutely suddenly and without even one minute of preceding senility.

This, then, was the man whom I remember for the first time when I was not quite six years old. We are in my mother's sitting-room at Elrig, and from the window we can see, at a distance of perhaps fifteen yards, a half-grown rabbit browsing upon some yellow garden plant. My mother, Aymer, Christian and myself – Eustace is absent. Uncle Willie imposed upon us children, probably by looks rather than words, complete silence and immobility. He held a twelve-bore shotgun, and millimetre by millimetre he slid the window up until the barrels of the gun could pass beneath. Then he shot the rabbit. The distance at which death had taken place was too great to disturb me; I identified myself with my uncle, not with the rabbit.

A few minutes later my brother Eustace, seven bouncing years old, entered on the line: 'I found a Carder Bees' nest in the terrace wall and I held the killing bottle over the entrance until I'd got the whole lot and then I only had to take one stone away to get the honey!' My uncle laid down the gun he'd been cleaning and said, very coldly and deliberately, 'Then you're a very cruel and destructive little boy, *aren't* you? If you were my son I'd beat you, and you'd never forget it.'

That was my very first remembrance of my uncle; his words hit virgin soil, and suddenly I felt for all the dead bees that had died in the killing bottle and the honey despoiled, and I felt guilt, massive and pervasive. I think he saw this, for insignificant as I was nothing was too small to escape his acute observation; perhaps he saw, too, that the soil was ripe for implantation, for from that very first remembered meeting he influenced me profoundly and lastingly. Identifying myself with his personality and his interests, I substituted for his unique collection of skins of Anatidae my own juvenilia; being young myself for the paraphernalia of taxidermy I entrusted to the cook the preparation of my collection of 'wings and tails'. These developed from the feathered appendages of roasting chickens and turkeys (oven-dried and reeking of salt and pepper) to those of wild game such as mallard or grouse, and by my sixth birthday the collection was in full swing.

'Sep. 16th, 1920

> 'Tynewood,
> 'Wylam,
> 'Northumberland

'Mother I hope you are having a nice time. Aunt Helen has sent us 4 wilde ducs and I am going to have the wings and tales. I have got a litel cold not much there was an flud yes-to-day it rose 15 feet there are trees rite out.'

Tynewood was my Aunt Victoria's house on the banks of the North Tyne, where for several years we often stayed both during the winters and when Elrig was let to summer shooting tenants. It was a bungalow, very isolated, and perched steeply above the road and the river; at the far side of the river ran a railway on whose track we would count the trucks of interminable goods trains. At Tynewood my aunt, always miserable unless working to the limit of her capacity, had started a chicken farm that was, by the standards of the day, intensive. The rooms were full of early incubators and the warm, oily smell of their heating lamps; these would glow in the dark like nursery nightlights and gave me a deep feeling of womb-like security.

I think she ran the whole enterprise with two employees, and did as much manual labour as either of them. The senior one, dignified by the name of manager, was called Dignan, and he had a fox-terrier who left a complete set of footprints across a huge yard of wet cement that was part of my aunt's constructional programme. These footprints are somehow concerned with an image of Tynewood that is essentially confused, because besides the happy and brightly coloured memories such as Humming-Bird Hawk Moths hovering over sweet williams, purple vetches among ferns on the drive bank, long days spent bird's-nesting in the habitual company of a boy colled Bobby whose father my aunt employed (I once said to Bobby as we munched our sandwiches by the sandy river's bank: 'Why don't you call me Gavin instead of Master Gavin?' And he was silent and awkward for a long minute

55

before he replied: 'Because it wouldn't be right.' I said: 'Then I shall call you Master Bobby', and to his great embarrassment when in strangers' company I always did); besides the happy journeys in my aunt's pony trap (upholstered like an old third class railway carriage, the pony's tail flicking at flies on her glossy chestnut crupper); besides all these things something sombre and terrible happened at Tynewood, something that returned to shatter me years later. I know objectively, because I have been told, what the incident may have been, but because I have no memory of it the fact should not find place here. More precise miseries I do remember.

At the far side of the concrete courtyard imprinted by the feet of Dignan's dog was the gateway to the wood and to the footpath that led up through it to the village on the ridge behind. From the gateway the path was flat at first, and for a hundred yards or so the post and rail fencing of the paddock lay at its left. The paddock had a little stream running through it, whose banks were made of stiff blue clay; where the arched and vaulted roots of a cherry tree formed Gothic caverns in the clay there lived a large toad to whom my sister and I would bring reverent offerings of worms. The toad and my aunt's pony seem the sole occupants of the big grass paddock, which, as I see it now, is in a perpetual dream twilight, or perhaps the hour preceding twilight, for while there is contrast between the colours of the blue clay, the smooth grey root bowls, the umber toad and the green grass, all these are of one tone, as though some benediction or curse were pronounced in a voice devoid of inflection.

One entered the paddock through a gate in the post and rail fencing. The gate hung from a heavy post some five feet high; my sister, four years older than my six years, used to climb to its top and jump down with a thudding squelch of gum-boots. She dared me to do the same. I clambered to the top, found myself too far from earth, and refused. She baited me until at last I said I would if she wasn't looking. I don't know whether I had any consciously formed plan of deception or whether I just just grown sick of her jeering and genuinely thought it would be easier if she wasn't there. Anyway, she promised not to look; she walked back down the path, into the concrete yard and out of sight. I considered the position from all angles, but I was much too far from the ground. I climbed down, stamped on the clay to make a noise like landing, and called to my sister that I had done it. She came round the corner with a look of blazing contemptuous triumph on her face, a look that made me almost dizzy. '*I* saw you!' she screamed, seeming quite beside herself in her excitement; '*I* saw you! You're not only a coward, you're a liar too!'

How many deliberate lies I had told in my life I don't know; probably few if any, for I was of almost morbidly tender conscience, but certainly this was the first time that I had ever been found out. My first reaction was despair and tears, my second a rising indignation that *she* had not kept her promise and yet dared to accuse me of breaking mine. 'You *looked*!' I yelled at her, jumping up and down with rage and frustration, 'You *looked*, and you *promised* you wouldn't! What right have *you* got to call *me* a liar?'

'That's quite different,' was all she would deign to reply. It was my first introduction to applied feminine logic; and it was a traumatic experience. We went and fed the toad in silence. On the way back the awful aura of the post reached out and engulfed me. I knew that nothing could make anything right now until I had really jumped off it. When I jumped my eyes were shamelessly shut and my sister's were shamelessly open. I landed on my backside in the mud.

My own rejection of logic was just as thorough if any of my taboos were touched upon. We were walking by the river-bank a hundred yards or so from the Wylham road. My sister pointed to some human excreta, topped by newspaper, and said:

'A tramp's been here.'
'It's not a tramp.'
'Well, what is it then?'
'Some kind of animal.'

'Then how did the paper get there?'
'It blew there, with the wind.'

It was at Tynewood that I remember the first of our long series of unusual pets. These were goats, and I think they belonged officially to my sister. At this distance of time I find it difficult to distinguish between individual goats in a line that spread over a number of years; they bore weird names such as Torfreda and Alftruda, reflections of my sister's schoolroom gothic reading, and they came for long walks with us, staying as close by as reasonably well-behaved dogs, browsing in the hedgerows, sometimes avoiding recapture with skittish flourishes of the heels, and occasionally munching a pocket-handkerchief.

At the same period Eustace owned a tame speckled bantam; supposed, when given to him by my aunt, to be a barely feathered female, he called it Mary, but when it started to crow some modification was clearly necessary so he renamed it Mary-the-Cock. It would perch on his arm or his shoulder as he walked about, and both it and Eustace were so proud of its unfeminine accomplishments that it learned to crow triumphantly at his command.

I think we must have been discouraged by my mother from burdening my aunt's household with too many strictly wild pets, for it is at Elrig, in the gun-room that contained the teeming by-products of my Aunt Muriel's entomological instruction, that I remember the unrewarding hedgehogs, the unweaned wild rabbits and the wood-pigeon squabs that would so invariably die; the young Tawny Owls, great blinking eyes and clicking bills in an amorphous mass of grey down like a powder-puff; the whole family of young rooks that would perch all over me like parasites wherever I went; and at Elrig the tame jackdaw that became our familiar for two years.

Aymer and I were looking for a Redshank's nest by a marshy little pool near the farm, when we saw this hopping, flapping black creature trying to make its escape among the rushes. The instinct for capture was always strong in us – the instinct that in late boyhood became a frankly predatory affair of guns and rifles and restored my father's gun-room to the purpose for which it had been designed – and calling excitedly to each other we set about cornering the creature much as two somewhat inept sheep-dogs might try their skill upon a very elusive ewe. The bird was like a piece of mercury, slipping through our grabbing fingers a hundred times before it was enclosed panting between Aymer's childish hands. I put my face to it, as I used to with all animals, and smelled for the first time the strange elusive, acrid tang of jackdaw feathers, a smell that I found and still find actively pleasant.

Jackie, as he (or she) was unoriginally named, was only just unable to fly, and, as my Aunt Muriel explained to us, was thus too old to become really and lastingly tame, but in this opinion she was wrong for once in a way. In a few weeks he had adopted us as his companions and playmates and Elrig as his playground. He lived completely free, and would come at call from his perch high on the crow-steps or the roof-ridge to alight on our shoulders with a delightful little chatter of pleasure; at mealtimes he would come in through the dining-room window and, sitting on a child's shoulder and leaning perilously forward, would try to intercept food between plate and mouth. He would steal and hide trinkets as jackdaws traditionally do, and it was this characteristic that was at length responsible for his death. One summer the house was let with the shooting to the Duke of Abercorn, whose butler, finding Jackie in the pantry and in the act of stealing a spoon, killed him. I remember that Aymer and I cried bitterly when we were told of it.

One of the stranger and more unlikely pets, coming later in the sequence, was a young heron. In the desolate, moon-encircled Mochrum Lochs were scattered rocky islands crowned with clumps of Scots pine, and one of these islands contained a strong heronry. Like the cormorant island on the most distant of the lochs, the heronry was highly odoriferous, detectable for a full half-mile downwind; landing, one found the ground and low vegetation beneath the trees to be as white with heron droppings as though hundreds of buckets of whitewash had been sloshed at random in every direction, and the stench of fish and eel remains fallen from the bulky nests above was overpowering. Though our quarry on this expedition was the chalky blue eggs for a collection that had by then grown to be the centre-point of our lives, the first nest to which I climbed contained three gawky youngsters, pot-bellied and scantily feathered. They sat upright, with all the length of their legs below the knee sticking out in front of them. Their faces were outraged, angry bright yellow eyes behind dagger bills and below an untidy mass of grey head feathers like hair standing on end. One of them leaned forward with a certain deliberation and emptied its crop of a large and partially digested eel, straight into my face. Despite this unendearing gesture of self-introduction we removed it from its nest (I think we chose that particular one because we knew it was no longer loaded, so to speak) and carried it home with us in the hope that it would become our close and constant companion. Its somewhat scantily clad body was no bigger than that of, say, a very small roasting chicken, but legs and neck were already attenuated, and the body was no more than a comic incident between toes and beak. At first it had difficulty in standing upright without wobbling, preferring to sit on its rump with legs outstretched before it, giving full prominence to its naked and slightly obscene belly, but after a few days it used to strut round after us like some ill-regulated piece of clockwork machinery on stilts, the mechanical effect heightened by an intermittent clattering of the mandibles that was its appeal for food.

My most vivid memories of the heron are after dusk. From the first we had the greatest difficulty in keeping it supplied with fish, for the nearest village with a shop, Port William, had long since ceased to be a fishing port; and the supplies arrived, usually already very ripe, from a fishmonger in Newton Stewart. The heron found nothing distasteful in this; and during the daylight hours, while it was free to march about the terrace garden, there was no visible evidence that its diet was not in prime condition. At night, however, we confined it for its own safety to a glorified rabbit hutch with a wire-netting front, and we fed it conscientiously immediately before our own bedtime. Looking back from the door of the house, content in the knowledge that the heron was replete and our duties fulfilled, we would see it shining like a beacon in the dark, the phosphorescence of putrescent fish glowing proudly through the thin and distended skin of its crop. The heron was an engaging and confiding creature, and we wept for it too when we were told that during our absence at school it had broken one of those long slaty grey legs and that there had been no alternative but to kill it.

The strange pet that survived the longest was not at Elrig, but at Northfield, the house at Albury that we shared with our Aunt Victoria when we were not in Scotland. It was an owl, and it was called Andrew. I found the nest high in a hollow tree, and it contained two tiny owlets no bigger than tennis-balls and as downy as powder-puffs. I took one and began the difficult descent; halfway down something nightmarish happened – I dropped the owl. I experienced such shattering remorse that I almost wanted to throw myself from the tree in expiation; I simply couldn't take in what Aymer was calling from the ground so far below – that the owl had landed in a pile of soft sawdust and was undamaged.

As Andrew grew and at last feathered, he became wholly confiding and inseparable from us. He would ride on the handlebars of our bicycles, or perch on our shoulders as we walked, preening our hair with little crooning sounds of affection, and like the jackdaw he would answer to his name, sweeping down on soundless wings from the leafy gloom of some great tree. He lived for three years, and was battered to death with a stick when, in our absence at school, he alighted on the push-handle of a pram belonging to a stranger, who believed the bird to be attacking the baby.

All our pets came to what are called bad ends, but the end of an animal is bad anyway, like the end of a human being, and through these extinctions we learned a little sympathy, a little understanding and a little compassion – things that could be transferred or extended to other human beings in later life. When we were small children my mother saw in us the will to care for and identify ourselves with these creatures even smaller than ourselves; and, wisely, she did not dissuade us by prophecy of the inevitable, though their perpetual presence and problems must have been an acute irritation. What she saw less clearly, perhaps, was the future impact of a crowded world of humans upon children who had known only animals and the adults of their own family.

4

SUBSTANCES AND SHADOWS

IT HAD BEEN, and remained for some years to come, my mother's practice to let Elrig for the shooting for the months of August and September, and to rent, usually in conjunction with some other members of her family, holiday accommodation for the children. Whether or not these transactions really showed any substantial profit I don't know. The last summer before I went to school we spent at a rented Surrey house called Wykehurst.

I remember very little of the house except that there was a large drawing-room on whose parquet flooring were scattered tiger skins with great stuffed heads over which one tripped constantly, and that we shared it with my uncle, Eustace Percy, and his wife Stella.

My Uncle Eustace, though a figure impressive enough to fill most canvases, made far less impact upon my childhood than Uncle Willie, for although of obvious goodwill and friendliness he had no interests that a child could possibly share. He was a politician and a man of enormous integrity, a combination so basically improbable that I understand it was no great surprise to his contemporaries when as a comparatively young man he retired from politics to become Rector of Durham University, and the first and last Lord Percy of Newcastle. Writing many years later, not long before his death, he defined his attitude towards his heritage. 'Born in 1887 with the biggest of all possible silver spoons in my mouth, and leaving Oxford in 1907 with something of the reputation of an infant prodigy, I seemed natural heir to the spaciousness of Edwardian and early Georgian England.... But "aristocracy", anyway, does not run to types, and its best fruits are apt to be a little out of season. A mild bent towards eccentricity and anachronism is, indeed, its virtue and its only salvation.'

At the time of which I am writing he was Minister of Education and MP for Hastings. He was as completely unlike the other surviving Percy uncles as my brother Eustace (his godson) was unlike Aymer or myself. The lean, beaky Percy bones were replaced by remarkable good looks of a more conventional order; he became portly in early middle age, though the cherub that his boyhood photographs show him to have been never quite disappeared. His walk was individual; he strutted, with great purpose, as though he were on perpetual parade, but the individuality of his step lay in the fact that he swung each foot into a central line, so that, like the Abominable Snowman, he would have left a linear set of prints, alternating left and right feet. His voice, doubtless modified by years of public speaking, boomed as though from somewhere far down in a great wooden wine-vat, and his laugh was mighty and Rabelaisian. Because, I suspect, of an unwillingness to clothe a thought in anything but the most precise words, he spoke with extreme deliberation, resulting either in embarrassingly long silences while he selected an adjective to his taste or, at a point where there was no natural caesura in his sentence, prolonged attempts to relight the pipe that he always smoked in informal surroundings. (I remember being impressed by the fact that he could afford these pauses; in my own family each would have been a raised portcullis inviting a babbling horde of invaders.) My Aunt Stella was six feet two inches in her stockings (we used to use her – in her absence – as a guide to linear measurement: 'Lay Aunt Stella out twice. No, three times'), beautiful, with a languid drawl and a highly *sympathique* substitution of w's for r's. How this rather splendid pair kept their tempers when our two households periodically united as they did at Wykehurst I have never understood; perhaps their protests were in private.

At Wykehurst I remember the dense green choking dustiness of cyprus trees as one climbed in search of birds' nests, bicycle rides to the Hurt Wood, where we waded through seas of magenta willow-herb in search of Hawk Moth caterpillars,

64

but the whole summer was overcast for me by the irrevoc-
ability of its end in school. I tried to ask my brothers what it
would be like, but they were secretive and offhand. 'You'll
soon see,' was the most terrifying reply, leading sometimes to
agonizing hours of lonely fear, and, 'Oh, you'll be all right, I
expect,' was the nearest I got to reassurance.

Educationally, I probably knew as much of dry and useless
fact, historical and geographical, as most children of my age;
but to these were added a vocabulary far in advance of my
years and an already partly formed handwriting. This vocabulary was due to reading adult books, and to an extensive – in
depth but certainly not in scope – knowledge of poetry. The
earliest reading I can remember was *Curdy and the Goblins*;
the narrative is lost to me now and only a few scattered images
remain. The strongest is, I think, composite, born of the book
and some private fantasy of my own – an hour-glass in a
moonlit attic, crystal for glass and stardust for the sand. By
the age of eight I had read all the magnificent animal stories of
Ernest Thompson Seton, together with a host of lesser bio-
graphers of wild creatures; in the following year I had read
all Baroness Orczy that were in the house, and then began on
the whole series of Stanley Weyman. My knowledge of a
limited field of verse was nothing short of prodigious; for besides being able to recite the greater part of *Lyra Heroica*, I
could also gabble my way with enthusiasm through much of
Macaulay's *Lays of Ancient Rome* (Lars – Porsena – of –
Clusium – by – the – nine – gods – he swore); Aytoun's *Lays
of the Scottish Cavaliers*; and (dutifully, for I didn't understand a word) ten full-length poems from *German Poetry for
Recitation*. I can still remember the bulk of all those things; I
cannot speak any German other than the words of the poems,
but I am told I speak them with a Swiss accent. I can only.
suppose that my mother must in her own childhood have had a
Swiss governess.

There were curious gaps in the slender library at Elrig;
there was not, for example, any of Shakespeare's plays or
poems, and by what must have been a chain of coincidences I

passed right through my school years without reading or hearing a word of Shakespeare, or even knowing the names of any of the obscurer plays.

As the beginning of the term drew nearer, I counted down the days. When the fatal time was only forty-eight hours away, I went to bed reciting to myself a little litany: 'Tomorrow it will be tomorrow and then the day will come'; and adding to my prayer, 'Oh Lord, let this cup pass from me, nevertheless not as I will but as Thou wilt.' I spent the last day making with a sort of wooden Meccano set a bookshelf for my collection of Stanley Weyman novels, as though I were entombing heroes whom I would never see again. The feel of those books is under my fingers now, limp red morocco and impressed gilt lettering. I arranged them in the sequence in which I had read them; *Under The Red Robe* at the right-hand end.

I do not remember the journey to school, nor why, it seems to me now, I did not travel in company with my brothers; perhaps I did, but in any case contact with them was lost so quickly that it would have made little difference. From the very first moment that I arrived at Heddon Court, Cockfosters, Barnet, I lived for that first term in a world of utter confusion, punctuated, as it were, only by moments of fear or humiliation greater than others.

I had by far greater reason for this state of mind than even the average child who went to school for the first time at the age of ten; the number of other children that I had met in my entire life could have been counted on the fingers of two hands, and of these all but my own family had been the most casual of acquaintances. Now I was thrown among an unthinkable number of boys, with whom I had seemingly nothing in common, and of whom by far the greater number appeared unequivocally hostile. From the beginning I was in a state of utter bewilderment that prevented me from carrying out the simplest action without somehow making a mess of it.

Heddon Court had one, but most certainly not more than one, sensible innovation to set against its appalling Baden-

Powell dictatorship, and that was the system called Substance and Shadow. A new boy, a Shadow, was, theoretically anyway, taken under the wing of an elder boy called his Substance, and for anything that the Shadow did wrong the Substance was punished. In some cases this led to a reign of terror by the Substance, who took out of his Shadow tenfold any punishment he himself received. I was lucky enough to be allotted an extremely nice Substance (though perhaps not so much luck as the headmaster's snobbery played the deciding role here – for we were the only children of titled parents) but even this in itself led almost immediately to confusion.

At some moment very soon after my mother had left, and my brothers, if they had ever been with me, had disappeared, a plump dark serious-looking boy came up to me and said: 'Maxwell minimus? I'm Simpson, your Substance. You're my Shadow. Better come for a little walk to the playing-fields now, and I'll explain things to you.'

He did his best, but it was all so strange, so extraordinary, that he might as well have been explaining the drill for ex- perimental space travel for all that I could take in. He covered a lot of ground; school rules, regulations for playing conkers (but I didn't know what conkers were, and was too shy to ask any questions), about not being a funk on the football field (but football was only a word to me), about not being cheeky to older boys ('including me – I'm twelve and a half and I've been here nearly four years'). It took the best part of half an hour, and as we walked back towards the school he said: 'If there's anything you want to know, just ask *me*, you see, not anyone else.' As an afterthought, he added: 'You're in one of the small dormitories, four people, and I'm one of them.' He stopped and looked embarrassed, then said very solemnly: 'When you're undressing and dressing in the dorm or the gym, all the fellows think it piggish if you show anything. You understand?'

Whether it was because this was the conclusion of his homily or because it appeared to touch upon some veiled, for- bidden subject, it was about all that had remained with me

67

when some two hours later we were in the dormitory. I needed no reminder; I had never felt shyer in my life. I had hardly got my pyjamas safely on, however, when he announced that it was our bath night, and led the way down the corridor into the bathroom. He pushed open the door, and immediately I found myself in a more terrible state of confusion than before. It may seem incredible, but it was the literal truth that never in my whole life had I seen a naked human being of either sex or any age – here were at least a dozen people with no clothes on at all, bathing, drying themselves, shouting and flipping each other with towels. I was so embarrassed that I couldn't find anywhere to look. Simpson came to my rescue. 'Hang your pyjamas up here and take that second bath from the end.' But the dilemma seemed to me appalling – if it was piggish to show anything when dressing or undressing, how much worse must it be to take off all one's clothes in front of a dozen people? Anyway, I didn't think I could do it. 'Come on,' he said, 'hurry up,' with a trace of impatience; and, undressing quickly, he hung up his own pyjamas. Left with no alternative but to undress, I was paralysed by the thought that it was possibly piggish to take off the top half first, or the bottom half first, and I hadn't noticed which he had done. 'Blank misgivings of a creature moving about in a world half realized' – world from which all landmarks seemed suddenly to have been removed.

In the bathroom that evening I was asked for the first time the question that was to torment all my schooldays afterwards, the question that led to my never learning to play tennis or voluntarily putting myself in any position in which I must expose my bare right forearm. 'What have you done to your arm, Maxwell?' I had five large strawberry birth-marks on the inside of the arm reaching from elbow to wrist. They became a symbol of shame before strangers, the most private part of my body.

There were, as far as I remember, only three boys' lavatories in the whole school; they were known as No. 1 place, No. 2

place and No. 3 place. Immediately after breakfast all boys formed a single line in queue; this was called 'lining up' and each boy called out as he left the lavatory, 'No. such and such place vacant,' and filed on downstairs. At the foot of the stairs stood the imposing St Trinians figure of the gym mistress, Miss Gib (brief blue tunic and vast columns of black-stockinged thighs), who challenged each boy as he passed, in the manner of a truculent sentry.

'Lined up, Maxwell minimus?'

Accustomed to choosing my own time for these things, and totally inhibited by the queue behind me from making any use of the lavatory, I could only reply, in a mesmerized way 'n-n-n-not properly, Miss Gib'.

'That is not my business, Maxwell minimus – for any matter concerning your health you should consult Matron during the eleven o'clock break.'

As I slunk away, nothing but my timidity curbed genuine curiosity as to the point of her question. If one had 'lined up' and nothing had happened, surely one must be unworthy of Miss Gib's scatological collection?

New smells and new tastes – all of them, with the exception of a round white sweet called sherbet balls, nauseating or unacceptable. Stale tobacco fear smell of Mr Stallard's study where I was beaten; bare wood board and sour boy-sweat stink of gymnasium; ammonia smell of the urinals; the sickening taste of liquorice sweets; rawness of mid-morning Bovril; disgust at undercooked smoked haddock at breakfast and cheap yellow curry for lunch.

The liquorice sweets I exchanged in quantity for a small flat pocket-torch with a protuberant magnifying bulb and imitation lizard-skin body. At either end of the body the metal top and bottom detached to give access to the battery and bulb respectively. The whole thing must have been smaller than I remember it, for measuring the perfect horseshoe-shaped scar that is still white on the knuckle of my left forefinger now, it is less than half an inch across. The end of the metal top slipped and cut deep into the flesh just above the knuckle, right in till it grated and slipped sideways on the bone. For a few seconds the bone showed dead white, then blood began to ooze out over it. It didn't hurt much, to have marked me for life.

I went upstairs to Matron's room, and while I was waiting for her to find a dressing I entered a dream that remained with me for many years. On the table was some boy's picture-book, and on the cover was a garishly painted polar landscape. In the foreground a polar bear stood heraldic on an ice-floe; the sea around it was deep blue, fathomless with secrets, and across the vast background of ink-blue sky flamed a stupendous curtain of multi-coloured aurora borealis. I was drawn into a majesty of icy desolation and loneliness, of limitless space and awful splendour, colder and remoter than the stars, so that my throat tightened and I wanted to cry because it was so beautiful and terrible. There were tears in my eyes when Matron came back and she thought it was because of the pain in my hand. The longing stayed with me, and when I first travelled alone, fourteen years later, it was to the Arctic that I journeyed.

I don't think I can have known, certainly that first term, where or how other boys spent what small leisure they had, for I was always mooching about in corridors or empty class-rooms, and always alone.

To me, pretending to read the notice-boards, or staring aimlessly out through rain-streaked window-panes at the dull December sky and the skeleton trees, would enter one Dunbar, a sweet and fatherly thirteen-year-old, who was a friend of my brother Aymer's. 'It's Maxwell minimus,' he would remark reflectively. 'Maxwell minimus, looking *rather* disconsolate.' (This precocity of speech seemed a feature of the school. We are standing in line for roll-call, our backs to the classroom wall. On my left is a boy called Holland minimus, black hair and chocolate-box colouring. As the headmaster enters the room I give Holland a terrific pinch. 'Take that back!' I hiss venomously. 'What?' he whispers. 'The bit about the abject fool?' 'No – the bit about the pathetic fallacy.' He had found out about our Church.)

My friendless and miserable state of affairs was almost immediately discovered by the only bully I had ever come across, a hideously ugly thirteen-year-old called Gartshawe. I can see him now, and hear the scuff of his loose heel-less slippers as he stalked me through the corridors, peering into empty classrooms in the hope of finding me cowering like a scared rabbit behind some open door. It was precisely there that I would often lurk, leaning against the wall and feigning to be absorbed in the book I carried, *The Red Cockade*, a small red cloth-bound book with a big ink-stain on the cover. Scuff, scuff, came the slippers down the corridors. They would pause outside the door, sometimes they would move on again, but this was only a refinement of cruelty, for he always knew where I was, and after a pace or two he would return to slouch round the door and confront me squarely. His face was so freckled that it seemed blotched; he had mouse-coloured hair, green eyes, a loose mouth and heavy round shoulders. He wore a baggy suit of Harris tweed, jacket and breeches, and the shapelessness of the outfit somehow made him seem more sinister, more unknown.

'Ah, Maxwell minimus. Your brother wants you in the gym.'

'Wh-which brother?'

'Maxwell major. He said you'd got to hurry. I'm going to give you a beaker, and if you don't hurry I'm going to give you two more.' (A beaker was a recognized Heddon Court form of aggression, the most violent pinch of which forefinger and thumb are capable, applied to the lower buttock. Properly delivered it was really painful and would leave a blue mark for at least a fortnight. As most of the smaller boys wore shorts it could without much difficulty be applied to the bare skin.) I scuttled off to the gym, holding back my tears as I passed through the long connecting glass corridor that smelled of boots and wet clothes. My brother was in the gym, talking to a boy I didn't know. I caught the end of a sentence '. . . and Shipton says he drives the Darracq at home.' 'Hallo, Maxwell minimus,' he said loftily. 'What do you want?'

71

'Gartshawe said you wanted me.'

'No,' said my brother. 'I don't want you,' and resumed his conversation.

Gartshawe was clever. He would alternate his inventions with genuine messages, and if I failed to comply with these he would deliver a 'flourish of beakers', which was still more painful and intimate. He was probably one of the few boys in the school who deserved the headmaster's standard punishment, a beating with a cricket-bat. (The first time my brother Eustace was so beaten he jumped up from the chair over which he was bent, shouting: 'Ow! That *hurt*!' He was quite right. The first time I was beaten I screamed at the second blow. '*I* don't think it's quite cricket,' said Dunbar – though it was rumoured that Mr Stallard had in fact once hit a ball by accident.)

This headmaster, H. Frampton Stallard, suffered from at least one – and probably at least one other less respectable – obsession. He bore a really extraordinary physical resemblance to Baden-Powell, and this unfortunate accident had set the blinkers firmly on eyes that I now fancy can never have been other than myopic. He worshipped the Scout movement with such an absolute fanaticism that not only did he believe it to be the moral duty of every boy to become a scout, but the moral duty of every grown man to become a scoutmaster before he became anything else. He must have appeared grotesque even to his own staff, but to us he was a figure of terror, and among so much that was simply unknown how could a ten-year-old detect the tragi-comedy contained in these fragments of his show day speech?

'The great phenomenon that first strikes us is the growth of the so-called Labour party, which in places at least is deeply tinged with the spirit of Communism. Now, when an ideal common to both rich and poor is proposed for our adoption, we must test it very carefully, and the test I apply is to ask whether this ideal is a fit one for a Christian Englishman. Tried by that test, it only needs to be started for it to be at once rejected. It was not in this way that our Empire was won.

I take it, therefore, as an Englishman, and much more as a Christian, that it is my first duty as a schoolmaster and equally yours as parents, to set before my boys the contrary ideal of service. I have left to the last the greatest agency in the promotion of this spirit, the Scouts. Now I used to think, and I still think, that so far as these boys of ours are concerned we could secure our object without "Scouting". But here comes in the point of the longer view which I commended to your consideration at the outset – the British Empire, and beyond that the Kingdom of Christ. How can our boys translate their virtue into terms of action? All our boys cannot be parsons, but my answer is that they may, and I hope they will, all be scoutmasters. That is what I hope for all our boys. They cannot be scoutmasters today, but ten years hence they can be. At that time they and I will no longer be enjoying the intimate relations which we now do, but you, their parents, will be. I ask you to remember what I say today in order that when that time comes you may remind your boys that *this* service is required of them, that they should lead a Troop of Scouts for England's sake – for Christ's sake.'

For Christ's sake!

(Mr Stallard was also District Commissioner of Scouts, and issued a bulletin on the 'First Cockfosters' Boy Scouts. 'The troop has been very active this term. Miss Gib, our Physical Mistress, has the knowledge which I lacked, and she is taking on the position of Assistant Scoutmaster and will obtain her warrant as soon as she has completed the three months' service with the troop which is an essential condition of office. Miss Stallard, my daughter, she too has been helping me in the matter of cooking, a subject of which I am profoundly ignorant.')

The consort of this curious caricature was no less egregious than he, though it was as if she had been battered into eccentricity by the horrible exuberance of his personality. She had a vague kindly face with thin bones and watery blue eyes; the generally shapeless figure made even more amorphous by the wearing of what I am still convinced was a small and slightly threadbare Oriental carpet round her shoulders – true it had a fringe, but of more rugged texture than ever graced a shawl. My brother Aymer saw her differently, as something purposeful, well able to direct her husband's life both to her comfort and profit. Long afterwards Aymer wrote of her: 'In giving him the school, Mrs Stallard had been both generous and shrewd. At one stroke she had provided herself with an income and an important part in his life, and her husband with fifty little scouts who, unlike toy soldiers, were a source of revenue and were changed at regular intervals before either they wore out or he had time to become bored with them.'

With the exception of Mr Malden (most schools possess a Mr Malden; his peacock presence, young, handsome, suave, well-dressed, a county cricketer or an ex-fighter pilot, usually possessing an expensive sports car, is necessary to emphasize the dowdy, poultry-like quality of his colleagues, who detest him because he steals the boys' worship while appearing indifferent to it) – with the exception of Mr Malden the staff were colourless, noticeable only by peculiar individual mannerisms, and by varying degrees of timidity or severity. Most of them, I imagine, would have made adequate scoutmasters. They were not alarming like Mr Stallard and our Physical Mistress, who possessed so intriguingly the knowledge that Mr Stallard lacked.

My mother visited the school towards the end of my first term and watched the boxing, a passion of Mr Stallard's second only to scouting. There was a lot of bleeding noses and blubbering little boys who managed to distribute whatever blood there was over every inch of their bare torsos and white cotton shorts, and to present pictures of such abject misery that my mother decided that I should not be taught to box. My brother Eustace was upset not so much by his bleeding nose and cut lip as by a deep sense of injustice; he had been disqualified for 'using his arms like a flail'.

It was an aspect of his ebullient and expansive personality. He would bounce and assert while I would skulk and hide; he was already feeding an image of himself while I was only

74

conscious of hostile externals. Aymer cast a sour spectacled eye upon the flapping and crowing of his fellow-nestling.

'Doody, I am afraid,' he wrote to my mother, 'is being frightfully extravagant with his money, he has spent more than three shillings already and he has written three letters to Miss Rose [my sister's governess] already within only nine days succession of each other, and he will not listen when I tell him that it would be much better to make all the letters into one envelope and under the same stamp. He uses up all his writing-paper with drawing moths and in all his letters there are at least four of them. He is drawing one now in his letter to you and you will probably see several more before he is finished. He sent a postcard and a letter off at the same time to Kish [my sister Christian] and the postcard had a penny ha'penny stamp on it because he did not happen to have a right kind of stamp. He is wasting a page of writing-paper now by not writing on both sides. He sends a lot of letters at the same time to the same person because "he says he likes to get a lot of letters off". Love from Aymer.

'Doody has just said that you told'

The letter ends there, mysteriously, as though Eustace had suddenly started using his arms like a flail again.

Eustace's letters to my mother during the same term were extrovert, expansive, describing some storm of which there is presumably other historical record. Anyway London seems to have survived the thousands of thunderbolts.

'My dear Mother,

'We have had the most terrible tropical thunder, the storm lasted for about several hours and starting at midnight, the hole sky looked as though it was on fire. London said that it was the worst storm that life in London had recorded. Thousands of thunderbolts fell all over London causing much damage, there was a more terrible fireball that fell too. Thursday night was the hotest night there has ever been in England I am alright again now and have been doing some work on Saturday there are only eleven more days till the holydays. Shall we be coming to Kings Cross and meet you there. What time will Miss Rose be able to come. I have made some sort of cigarette things which you light and hold in your hand and it gives a kind of smoke so as to keep the miges off, they are for the holydays. With love from Eustace.'

During my year at Heddon Court I made my first friend and my first enemy of my own age, each with the wholehearted intensity of an utterly new experience.

After my first term I had been moved from the foursome dormitory, under the benign eye of my Substance, to a two-bedded room which I shared with my enemy, giving the maximum possible opportunity for full development of the relationship, not only on rising and retiring but during a period of each day which we were intended to spend resting. Studley was an odd little boy with a face somehow like a clown's mask; bat ears, a very pale freckled skin, round angry brown eyes, and halfway up a high forehead a pair of half-circular eyebrows. It was not only their shape and position that made these eyebrows remarkable, but their extraordinary mobility; while under the influence of anger – which, like a lemming, was their owner's habitual mood – they shot up and down like the pistons of a high-revving engine. Whatever the cause of our original quarrel the feud, once established, was wholly self-sufficient and self-perpetuating; it required no pretext of renewal, and once that dormitory door was closed behind us it needed no more than a challenging wriggle of those eyebrows and we were hard at it again. Studley had set the style of fighting on the opening day, and it never varied throughout all its interminable rounds – it was a face-slapping match. Only the right hand was used to attack, the left being purely defensive, so that the opponent's left cheek was in fact the only target. We fought in silence. Up and down that little room we would prance, light on our feet like boxers, Studley's eyebrows leaping like dolphins, our right cheeks pale with rage and our left stinging and scarlet. Nothing but the sound of the bell, or of footsteps in the passage, could bring the fight to a temporary close. Outside the dormitory we ignored each other completely; our mutual hatred had no other form of expression. We were caught once, by the Matron, and Mr Stallard beat us both with a No. 4 cricket-bat on our bare buttocks, in his horrible pipe-smelling study, but neither of us found in the incident any excuse for *rapprochement*, and that evening, after an almost formal viewing of each other's bruised behinds, we were at it again.

All this seemed no stranger to me than any part of this mad life that bore no relation to any of my realities. When I groped in my mind for sanities and certainties, it was to the images of my mother and of Elrig that I would turn; I had to exclude my brothers, for they were there at Heddon Court with me, part of the nightmare, activated by unguessable motives that I could never share. My mother and Elrig were secure, even though the other boys had seized on the name and rechristened it the House of Earwig.

In all this confusion, issues required to be simplified, and it was probably as necessary to me for my relationship with Studley to be all enmity as it was for that with Heisch to be all love. I do not remember meeting him for the first time, only, with an extraordinary vividness, our reunion after he had been away from the school for a time. His elder brother, a friend of Aymer's, was a musical prodigy and a boy of striking appearance, very much older than I, whom I saw only from a distance; it is possible that this senior partnership may have intentionally fostered a junior alliance between the two families. My Heisch – if I ever knew his Christian name, which I doubt, I've forgotten it – did not come back at the end of the Easter holidays, for he had broken his leg skating and was in hospital at Eastbourne. Without him, during the first fortnight of that summer term, I was utterly desolate, and so completely did love cast out fear that I actually stopped Mr Stallard in the passage and asked him when Heisch was coming back. He seemed amused and quite benign and promised that I'd be told as soon as anything was definite. A few days later, a Sunday, I was told by Matron that Heisch was coming back that day, and that I was to wait behind in the dining-room after lunch. I waited, at the far end of the long room where I'd been sitting, and presently I saw from the window boys setting off in twos carrying tartan rugs, books, magazines, chess and draught sets, to spend the afternoon lying in the sun on the lawn. After a long time I heard Matron's voice outside the door; then she threw it open and held it open for Heisch. For a moment he stood there quite motionless on crutches, a statue unveiled, then very slowly and painfully he began to swing himself towards me. I didn't go forward to meet him – remembering, I seem never to have produced the conventionally expected or appropriate response to any situation – but stood up and faced him and waited where I was at the distant table so that he had the whole length of the room to cover on his crutches, swinging his stiff right leg encased in plaster of paris to the knee below his grey flannel shorts. I was experiencing so intense and active a happiness that for me there was no adequate way of expressing it. I just stood there and smiled and blushed, and then the smile became a grin, and he grinned too and blushed as deeply as I, and neither of us said a word during the long minute he took to cross the room.

Writing now, his boy face comes back into so sharp a focus that I find it difficult to realize that if he is alive he is a middle-aged man whom I should not recognize. If I had been asked to describe him in those days I should probably have been able to think of no salient features but the unusual colour of his hair and his arrestingly white and even teeth, for I did not think of people's features in detail, only of a general impression or aura that was almost always at once favourable or unfavourable, rarely negative. His hair was red, but unlike any red I have seen before or since; it ranged through very dark red where it was short at the nape and the temples, to pale flame at the forelock, and while it was very fine it was also very springy, so that it became spiky and untidy within seconds of being brushed. Eyebrows and eyelashes were dark like the nape hair, and his eyes were a piercing transparent blue without any hint of green. The features of his oval face were straight and regular, of a curious perfection, and when he smiled as he was smiling now his teeth were snow-white against clear lips and skin.

He reached my table, flushed and panting slightly.

'Hello, Earwig,' he said softly.

'Hello, Phoenix.' I had invented this name for him because of his hair.

He sat down, arranging his splinted leg in front of him with difficulty. We went on looking at each other and grinning. For some reason he accorded to me the same unstinted devotion as I did to him; we were wholly happy in each other's company, and words were of no particular importance. I had an orange in my pocket; we divided it into 'pigs' and ate it slowly. Later, we took rugs out on to the lawn and read.

That night I fought Studley with renewed zest.

Heisch would have made Heddon Court tolerable, he was a certainty, the only certainty I had found away from home, but I and my two brothers all left Heddon Court for ever before the end of that term.

There was an epidemic of scarlet fever and the majority of parents removed their children for the few weeks that remained. Aymer was in any case going on to Eton in the autumn, and my mother, feeling that neither Eustace nor I were progressing as we should, decided to send us elsewhere. It was the beginning of a policy of dispersion; never again did she have all her eggs in one basket, or chickens in one coop, and it was another fourteen years and the beginning of the Second World War before I again found myself a member of the same institution as one of my brothers.

I contrived to feel romantic and sentimental even about leaving Heddon Court. At my last evening prayers we sang the hymn that always stirred my hyper-emotional nature to tears.

'Far, far away like bells at evening pealing . . .' and the drab school-smelling classroom was gone and I was in a summer sunset landscape where parkland trees cast long shadows on the ripening corn below an apple-green sky, and lights pricked the gathering haze in the valley below. So I spent my last night at the school as I had spent my first, in tears – for Heisch perhaps, or for the curtain that school seemed to have set between Aymer and myself, or for the destructive sense of insufficiency that a child feels when it fails to measure up to a new and incomprehensible set of rules and standards. I was alone, because Studley had scarlet fever.

5

ST WULFRIC'S

THE NEXT preparatory school chosen for me after our mass exodus from Heddon Court has been described by Cyril Connolly in *Enemies of Promise*, and as he chose to write of it as St Wulfric's and is clearly a better hagiologist than I am, St Wulfric's it can remain. In any case it is long dead, burnt to the ground, and like Heddon Court the almost rural tract of land on which it stood is densely built over, part of the town of Eastbourne, so that there is nothing left to recall the pangs and fears of long ago.

When I went there at the age of eleven Cyril Connolly and his school-fellows George Orwell and Cecil Beaton had left it nearly ten years before (a vintage era, that), yet it is not the changes, the dissimilarities, between his St Wulfric's and mine that are striking, so much as the complete lack of evolution apparent during that decade; and the reason for this was clearly the existence of one wholly dominant personality.

The headmaster and his wife were known as Sambo and Flip – or rather, to put it quite bluntly at the outset, the headmistress was called Flip and her husband Sambo, for St Wulfric's was a strictly matriarchal culture and the existence of an assertive male at the summit of the hierarchy would have been unthinkable. Sambo's headmastership was a courtesy title only; I think he taught some of the senior forms, he caned boys when ordered to do so by Flip, put his signature where he was told to, and got up early enough every morning to watch ninety naked and shivering little boys take their regulation cold plunge in the swimming-bath. He spoke little, was inclined to mumble, and was said to spend most of his time playing golf. (The only time he ever beat me he absentmindedly picked up a steel-shafted driver instead of a cane, and terrifying shades of Mr Stallard's cricket-bats swirled through my mind. Did all schoolmasters use the implements of their personal sport? Hockey . . . polo . . . but he collected himself in time and chose with some care a green cane resembling a small trout rod. *Vive le sport*.)

'Flip, around whom the school revolved,' wrote Cyril Connolly, 'was able, ambitious, temperamental and energetic. She wanted it to be a success, have more boys, to attract the sons of peers and send them all to Eton. . . . When angry Flip would slap our faces, in front of the school, or pull the hair behind our ears, till we cried. She would make satirical remarks at meals that pierced like a rapier, and then put us through interviews in which we bellowed with repentance. . . . On all the boys who went through this Elizabeth and Essex relationship she had a remarkable effect, hotting them up like Alfa Romeos for the Brooklands of Life.' She failed to hot me up; perhaps I was unhottable, and certainly I was desperately unpromising material for her particular techniques.

The appearance of Flip, her gestures – from her mannish way of lighting and smoking constant cigarettes to her purposeful walk – her voice, sharp with anger and sarcasm or jolly and encouraging, dominated every corner of St Wulfric's. She was a stout woman in middle age, with a well-developed bust from which her nickname was derived. (There was a curious schoolboy slang word for breasts at St Wulfric's that I have never heard before or since; phonetically 'wilybers'; 'here comes Flip,' someone would say, 'wilybers flapping nicely, eighty to the minute, everything in clockwork order'.) She carried herself very straight and all her movements were sharply positive. She had grey hair, dark brown eyes that became absolutely opaque and round when she was angry, and she generally wore brown clothes.

She had favourites (as in Cyril Connolly's day, to be 'in favour' or 'out of favour' made the difference between a just tolerable life and a perfect hell; 'for, womanlike, Flip treated the very being out of favour as a crime in itself, punishing us for the timid looks and underdog manner by which we showed it') and, naturally enough for a woman both emotional and ambitious, her favourites were initially chosen sometimes for their charm or their qualities and sometimes for their influential background. There was only one other boy at St Wulfric's whose parents had what Flip called, with varying intonation, 'a handle to their names', and he chanced to be a boy of such stupefying good looks as to present Flip with the irresistible combination – like certain TV advertised detergents he was the best on the market because he was the only one to have *two* ingredients *never* combined before. He never fell from favour during my two chaotic years at St Wulfric's, a record surpassed, I think, only by two brothers whose parents had sent a whole litter of male pups through St Wulfric's and signified their appreciation of the result by donating funds for a new wing to contain a library.

Flip would have liked to have kept me in favour but I was just too much of an oddity for a busy woman to cope with. She started to do her best the day after I arrived, which was either a Sunday or for some other reason a holiday. She took me, another boy (already dressed in our regulation green jerseys and corduroy breeches that rubbed with a purring noise as we walked) and her daughter Robina, all of an age, to go blackberry picking. We packed into her Willys Knight (two-seater and dickey, all painted in two shades of brown) and drove off up the chalk downs and parked the car and wandered in briarchoked disused farm lanes where the chalk was everywhere like dirty snow underfoot and there was sunshine and big white cumulus clouds blowing on the early autumn wind. We filled our baskets with blackberries, and Flip gave us cake, and coffee from a Thermos; it ought to have been a wonderful start, and I don't see what more she could have done, but it didn't work because I was outside my environment and I behaved as an animal does in the same circumstances. I couldn't produce the right responses, and so I shrank. I had never been in the company of a girl of my own age (and Robina was in any case most unlike my sister), and I didn't know how to address Flip. Several times I tried to say her whole name 'Mrs Brunt', but because of my uncertainty about whether this was the correct form of address I stuck on the first syllable, so that it came out as 'Miss'. The other boy muttered to me: 'Don't say Miss, say Mum'; and this made my dilemma ten times worse. I had heard of the word 'mum' as something other people called their female parent (I had been brought up to call mine 'Mother') and because I had met so few people I just did not know that 'Mum' was the respectful way of, say, a servant addressing his mistress; I had never stayed in other people's houses, and the servants at home called my mother 'M'lady'. So when I tried to call Flip 'Mum' the image became utterly confused; I might as well have called her 'O Queen', or 'Little sister of all the world' for all the reality the sound represented. Flip must already have been becoming irritated by me at the end of that first afternoon, but she had not yet irritated me.

This happened during the first Sunday letter-writing period. It was Flip's custom to invite her favourites, or those otherwise in need of special surveillance, to write their Sunday letters home in the comfort of her big oak-lined cigarette-smelling sitting-room. (Brown plush cushions in brown leather armchairs and sofa.) This was, in fact, an indirect censorship; Flip inspected the quality of the handwriting, and this inhibited the writer from setting down anything but the most vapid sentiments of contentment. This would have been cause enough to start in me a helpless, childish resentment, but there was worse. I already had a precocious cursive handwriting, which apart from a few experimental decorations such as Greek e's, soon discarded, differed very little from what it is today. It was also fast – a word would take me as little time as would a single letter of my contemporaries' separated script, which I found out on that first Sunday to be compulsory at St Wulfric's – or at least in the inner circle of Flip's Sunday letter-writing group. I was made to write out the whole thing again, each letter well separated from the next. It was much worse than having had to undress for the first time at Heddon Court; it seemed to me more unnecessary and more gratuitously insulting.

It had other repercussions. For minor offences our form

masters would set us lines to write out – 50 or 200 according to the gravity of the offence or the state of the master's temper at the time. These would take me a matter of minutes, while the same number would take another boy – possibly given the same punishment at the same time – hours of laborious work. This made me unpopular; it seemed to them that I had an unfair advantage, and so one of my very few accomplishments became at once a handicap, a piece of witchcraft to be indicated and punished by fellow-prisoners. And because they resented this one achievement that meant so much more to them than to me, they displayed resentment in many ways; mocking the birthmarks on my arm, my inability to swim or to box, the fact that my mother had a 'handle to her name'; that my uncle was Minister of Education – they all became targets. The fact was that I was inefficient at the things most boys do adequately without much help, and suspectly clever at individual skills that seemed to me to need no learning. I could draw and paint, sprint a very fast 100 yards, write fluently, and was actually top scorer on the miniature rifle range (for which I was beaten up by my unsuccessful fourteen-year-old rival, son of a famous motor racing driver). But my insecurity, my absolute lack of landmarks, made me stupid and uncertain in everyday life, gauche and awkward with grown-ups and weakly defensive with contemporaries. I had lived in a very small group; I was frightened, as I had been at Heddon Court, of numbers. If a dozen people had said that my skin was green I would have believed them, and it seemed that they said many more things at least as disturbing.

Below the steam-rolling level of Flip there remain clear-cut remembrances of both masters and boys, but very few considering how many there were of both. Mr Marvel was the Mr Malden of St Wulfric's, the dazzler whom almost every boy admired and wanted to be like in the future. He was a tall, handsome, debonair young man in his mid-twenties with blue eyes and a fair moustache cut *en brosse*. He possessed an almost inexhaustible wardrobe and a vast collection of coloured silk handkerchiefs on which he would actually blow his nose the better to display one before returning it to an even more flamboyant protuberance from his breast pocket. ('I wish I could put them in like Marvers', I can still hear the breaking voice of a senior admirer say.) Boys competed to count the number of specimens observed; the highest score claimed and reluctantly admitted by rivals was forty-seven. The silk shirts didn't yield to such analysis, because they were all almost exactly the same. He could raise one eyebrow almost to the hairline while the other remained absolutely motionless; this was his invariable reaction, while he wrote or read, to a raised hand and a treble voice calling 'Sir!' in his classroom. He owned the inevitable sports car, but with a touch of vulgarity which, while it jarred my precocious susceptibilities, enhanced the general atmosphere of insolence that endeared him to other small boys. He had two successive cars while I was at St Wulfric's; both were two-seater MGs, the first bull-nosed and the second square-nosed; both were of highly polished aluminium with red mudguards and red leather upholstery, and both had a name painted in gold letters along the side on the bonnet. I suppose the name might have been even worse than it was – might, for instance, have been Meteor, or Silver Lightning, or even Shooting Star, but it needn't have been placed between quotes as were the actual words 'MYRA' and 'MYRA II'. Needless to say the mascot from the first car was transferred to the second and needless to say it was a naked woman, in the act of diving, with her plump polished buttocks thrust well back towards the driver.

He played rugby football, possibly for the county, but certainly for eminent clubs, and I can see him lying at length on the big plush sofa in Flip's sitting-room, having his long hairy thigh massaged after some fierce game ('Ronnie played like a tiger,' said Flip) in which his injuries enhanced his reputation. His whole personality, which I imagine to have been neither particularly great nor particularly small, had an extraordinary, almost hysterical, impact upon the boys. Early one Easter term he returned a week or two late to St Wulfric's, having broken his leg while ski-ing in Switzerland, and the first that we saw of him was when he entered and walked the length of the dining-room, just after we had sat down to lunch. He was, as I have said, tall, perhaps six feet two or three, and this presumably made his limp the more noticeable, for he could put no weight at all upon one foot. The room fell absolutely silent as he entered; then, as he hobbled down the length of it between the tables, all the way to where Flip and Sambo were sitting at the far end, a long sighing whistle of awe and dismay rose and swelled from the lips of his worshippers, the voice of those who see their god bitterly wounded in battle but defiant and glorious still.

Mr Marvel was a phenomenon to be observed and wondered at; a bright light from which a boy's innate desire for exhibitionism caught a reflected flash, as our still smooth metal angled to his sun's beam. But though he was kindly and even-tempered, rarely displaying the morning hangover that I now suspect to have been a commonplace, he was wholly indifferent to boys and thus had little lasting impact upon them. They would worship him for a while and then move on to their public schools and find another playing the same character part and transfer their allegiance to him for a time and at length go a whoring after other gods.

Mr Ellis was of very different potential. There were two masters called Ellis; the one of whom I am writing was known as Egg, because of his absolutely hairless cranium. In Cyril Connolly's time he appears to have been called Daddy Ellis, but when I was at St Wulfric's he was known only as Egg, and the other Mr Ellis was called The Other Mr Ellis, whether or not Egg was part of the conversation. From what I remember of The Other Mr Ellis he was colourless enough to justify this distinction by anonymity.

Egg was stocky and middle-aged, with a very large smooth skull and face, on which the only incidents were large pale grey eyes and a stubbly sand-coloured moustache. He dressed in very baggy light brown plus-four suits and highly polished brown shoes, invariably carried a walking-stick which he never used for walking with, and taught mathematics by uncon-

ventional means. Whether his tantrums were real or feigned
they were highly impressive. Failure by an individual to give
the correct answer to a question was enough to start a ten-
minute seeming manic hysteria, beginning with a terrifying
crash of his stick across the culprit's desk, a crash that would
have broken bones unwise enough to be in the way. 'Your
parents, Marsden, are paying gold – *gold*, Marsden, for every
minute you sit here in this classroom. They are paying *gold*
(*crash*) for one of the best mathematics teachers in the world to
hammer into your wooden skull how to earn a living when you
grow up.' (*Crash*.) Then he would leave Marsden and the stick
would lash at every desk in the room. 'Do you understand, all
you rabbits on whom I am wasting my time and my life – yes
my *life* (*crash* – *crash* – *crash*) – that unless you listen to me
and learn from me you will die of *starvation*? You will end as
the cavemen you *deserve* to be.' Flailing round him, his stick
lands with a colossal thwack across my desk, bouncing the
silver half-hunter watch that was my last birthday-present and
which I can't bear to let out of my sight. The whole mood
changes, and apparently with no sarcasm, no irony, though I
am quite the worst pupil in his class : 'I *beg* your pardon, sir, I
beg your pardon,' and his face is gentle and solicitous. 'When a
man's angry he doesn't always know who he is hitting at. It
was *not* my intention to hit you, sir, *or* your desk, *or* that
beautiful watch. You call me "sir" because I am worthy of
respect; *I* call *you* "sir" because I think *you* are worthy of
respect. Pardon me, sir, please.' This would elicit a titter from
the rest of the class which would start the full tantrum and the
stick working again. Because I had not enough *savoir-faire* to
run with the hare and hunt with the hounds, it was I who
suffered from Egg's alliance; each time that I was singled out
for notice I was driven further from the fold of the herd,
further from any possibility of assimilation.

It had been my mother's intention – very advanced for those
days – to prepare us for a democratic society by sending us to
schools which, though upper middle class in background, were

not traditionally aristocratic. She had shunned such prep schools as Summer Fields because there we should have consolidated precisely the titled privileges and grandeur from which she herself had actively escaped; the greater number of boys with whom we consorted would have been from the backdrop of Burke or Debrett's columns. She was anxious that we should learn to get on with boys who, though possibly of prosperous families, were not of a particular clique. It was admirable in concept, but as with most social reforms the generation in question had to suffer in proportion with the magnitude of the aims. Thus I was not murdered or executed as effete; I was singled out as a target for jealousy by those whose parents would have liked a 'handle to their names' and whose status-symbol cars compared spectacularly with the modest and practical conveyances my mother chose. There was no escaping the fact that I was the odd-man-out, or that I was not robust enough to cope with the situation.

Of a young master, who I think was called Mr Gumbles, and taught me history, I remember a very few things, but very vividly. He played no games, had a gaucho black moustache and an oddly long stride, and in retrospect I realize that he was extremely unsure of himself. On a weekly history test, he loped up to the blackboard and wrote his first question 'Who beat De Gras?' This struck me as a funny and naïve simplification of the issue, and though I probably didn't know the answer then and certainly don't know it now (or even who De Gras was) it was one of my first recognitions of weakness, woolliness. My only other recollection of him was of a question concerning one of my ancestors, probably Harry Hotspur. As usual I did not know the answer. He came diving down the desks from his rostrum, bubbling with an almost indecent excitement. '*You* ought to know,' he said. '*You* ought to know – he was one of your *ancestors*! You can at least know your *family* history!' This only made the oher boys more anxious to draw comparisons between my plainly pugnacious ancestors and pacific self; what kind of princeling was this that was being praised? He had neither the remoteness nor the prowess to justify himself; he was just a wet little boy who was obviously easily bullied by any one of the recognized techniques.

This situation was made very much worse by the appearance in *Punch* of a whole-page cartoon of my two uncles Alan Northumberland and Eustace Percy as charging knights on horseback, above the caption, 'The Percys in action, or, as some say, reaction.' I was far too young to understand the word reaction, or to appreciate the issue of coal royalties (Uncle Alan was the greatest mine-owner in the British Isles) upon which the attack was based, but I did know that for days after this boys whom I didn't know would thrust this picture in front of my nose and make unintelligible – but clearly derogatory – remarks. I have not seen the cartoon for an unthinkable number of years, but I can recall much of its detail with a feeling of fear and confusion. I was supposed to understand what all this controversy was about, but I hadn't got the vaguest idea, and didn't want to have. When the pretty red-haired twenty-year-old matron's assistant said to me, 'Tell Lord Eustace that there's no Trade Unions where *I* come from,' I asked with absolute sincerity, 'Would he be interested?' – but she took this for an intentional impertinence, and would not speak to me for several days. In fact, nobody had ever told me what a Trade Union was, and why should they?

There was one master whose real goodness I recognized, but either he was too weak, or I was too inaccessible, for him to pull me out of what had by then become a ditch of unhappiness. He taught geography and art, and I remember him as one of the few people in my whole life of whom I can think without analysis or criticism. Mr Sillar must have been about sixty then, a devoted naturalist and a devoted paedophile; he loved us all with an all-embracing affection, and fanned in each one of us the least spark of being that he could understand. He taught drawing ('Now you've got the outline right, line it in firmly and carefully – don't leave it muzzy' – even

THE PERCYS IN ACTION
(Or, as some say, Reaction).

Mr Sillar unknowingly carried into his teaching the funda-
mental message of St Wulfric's) and looking over his shoulder,
watching him add the hard black uncompromising edges to
tentative shapes, I was absorbed with the broad diamond
pattern of wrinkles on his neck, wrinkles that would change
shape as he moved, like expanding wood rose trellis. He taught
geography too, and because of that there arose a long misunderstanding in my mind about caviare. He was dealing with
the Caspian Sea, and telling us of the importance of the

caviare industry when he suddenly jumped up and said: 'Oh, I forgot to give you all a taste of caviare!' – and passed round a box of expensive *fondant* sweets. Whether any other of the class clung for several years to the illusion of a sturgeon who laid huge conical sugary eggs flavoured and coloured with various fruits I don't know, but I did.

When I finally left St Wulfric's in a quaking jelly of misery and self-pity, he said: 'Just remember your luck will change – and never give up your interest in natural history,' and a little later he sent me his whole collection of bird skins from which he had been used to teach us to paint. We were still corresponding in a desultory fashion ten years later, and he had such faith in me that I wish he had lived to see any form of the success that he so doggedly predicted.

He nurtured and fostered my interest in natural history ('no one can understand difficult things like their own lives and other people unless they understand simpler things like animals and birds first') during my two years at St Wulfric's; so that during the holidays, when I was restored to my normal existence in the family, it became my centre-point, and the point at which Aymer and I fused. Life at school and life at home – the almost uniformly unhappy apathy of St Wulfric's and the deep uncomplicated contentment of the holidays – were so utterly unrelated that it seems now as if they must have run parallel in time and been lived by two different people, rather than in their true alternating sequence. I remember that at the time I used to think of life like telegraph wires watched from a train window – in the holidays they would soar up until it seemed they would climb the sky, only to be inevitably slapped down by the next telegraph post – the term.

Elrig, with the spring wind on the moors and the music of the curlews, with the blanket of the daffodils blowing in the sunshine on the slope before the house and the rooks calling about their nests in the clump of elms beyond – Elrig was all that I or Aymer would recognize as home. Each of us would carry with us to school some small memento of our high, wild upland; a sprig of white heather or of fragrant bog myrtle, even a little piece of peat from the big rush peat-basket beside the terrace-room fire, as those older than we were cherish a lover's letter or a lock of hair. Coming home by railway from the south, the first landmark was breakfast in the Station Hotel at Dumfries (porridge and fried whiting, the fish's tail ingeniously stuck into its mouth), then the branch line with its tiny, sleepy moorland stations beyond New Galloway, where the hiss of escaping steam would mingle with the clucking of the stationmaster's hens, and there were rambler roses on the station buildings; then a long stretch with nothing but hills and heather and the gleam of moorland lochs, a stretch that ended at Gatehouse of Fleet, where on the bank beside the platform the name of the station was written in cockle-shells and bordered by sweet williams, and pouter pigeons crooned upon a white dovecot. This was my gatehouse, the gatehouse to my home; I played with the word, turning it over in mouth and mind until the sound itself became a symbol of hope.

When we travelled north by road it was a very much longer process, a fore-pleasure spun out. We would set off from the south, packed tight into whatever was our car of the moment (T-model Ford, bull-nosed Morris Cabriolet, and later, for some reason I never understood, vintage Studebakers), and take at least three days over the journey. There was a chauffeur at the wheel, liveried to disguise his eccentricities of rudeness, individuality, madness, criminality or plain inefficiency, and we would arrive, usually late, at some destination such as Norman Cross or Barnby Moor after a day's drive of a hundred miles or so. We had picnic lunches, and from the high hawthorn hedges of the Midlands, Aymer and I would carry home specimens of thrushes' or blackbirds' eggs the more precious for being filched from the enemy territory of England, plunder carried home by conscripts of an army in retreat.

Although the house was always let to shooting tenants in the summer holidays, and so for a few years it was only at Easter that we were there, Elrig enshrined our whole beings, our thoughts and our happiness. It enshrined too, our almost obsessively important collection of birds' eggs – known succinctly as 'the collection' and by then occupying many pretentious cabinets in a room all their own, a little walled-off section of 'the unfinished rooms'. The insect collecting had not quite stopped, and the sight of some rare and gaudy species would still stir us to activity, but wave they their wings or legs never so gaudily they could not compete with the hypnotism of the eggs, so ovoid and so infinitely variegated, so well-concealed and cherished both before and after their reduction to captivity. We could not have loved them more if we had laid the lot.

The collection had received a tremendous stimulus from a chance meeting with a grown-up collector, owner of one of the largest egg collections in the world. (He also collected stamps and regimental buttons, and something else that I have forgotten, but eggs were the heart of the matter.) The fact that he lived three miles over the hill and that we had never heard of his existence was no more than one of an aggregate of improbabilities that composed our own.

The rough hill land that stretched away on all sides from Elrig was sprinkled here and there with shaggy fir and larch plantations surrounded by crumbling dry stone walls, and planted for some reason long forgotten, for they were neither thinned nor tended. Many trees had blown; they would lie with their turf-grown roots choked with bracken and briars, the limbs of some fallen larch grown over with a thick hairy grey lichen, the whole as nearly impenetrable as the barrier of interlaced sitka twigs in the gloom of standing trees beyond them. To these jungles Aymer and I would come looking for the nests of hawks and owls and jackdaws (in case any ornithologist should think he detects an error here, Galloway jackdaws nested habitually in the fir trees, vast nests that grew larger with every generation, so that sometimes they formed an obstruction that a climber could not pass, and owls used the un-tenanted nests). Early one Easter holidays we bicycled farther afield than usual and began to explore a large wood, a little less battered and shaggy than the hill-side spinneys. We had spotted a hawk's nest, and I already had hand and foot on the lowermost branches of the tree when Aymer said: 'There's a man coming!' I turned, and in the muted light of the fir wood I saw the most extraordinary person approaching us over the pine-needle carpet. It was a man all right, but a very unusual one, for at the most he was some four-and-a-half feet high. He had a big head and broad shoulders, but from the waist down-wards he might have been a boy of fourteen or so. He was dressed in a baggy tweed jacket, tweed breeches and heavy brogues; he had grey hair and a clipped grey moustache. He held his head low and thrust forward, and then as he turned to avoid some obstacle we saw that he was a hunch-back. He stopped in front of us and said in an odd voice that had some-thing like a giggle in it: 'Morning. Who are you?' And then, before we could answer: 'This is p-p-p-private p-p-p-prop-erty!' Aymer (who also had an impediment in his speech, but fortunately of the hesitant, gasping kind) managed to say: 'I'm sorry, we didn't know. Who does it belong to?' The apparition grinned, although the effort of preparing the next sentence made the grin more like a mild snarl. 'M-m-m-me! I am the p-p-p-proprietor! Where are you from?' As all his breath had been used in the machine-gun fire of the main word, the final question was spoken on the intake of the next, and was almost inaudible. (As we got to know him better, we became familiar with further departures from normal speech that were habitual to him; all of them imposed by the initial consonant stammer that used up his magazine of breath before the word-target was fairly in his sights. A polysyllabic word such as Barnbarroch, the name of a neighbouring estate, was clearly an impossibility if, even starting with full lungs, the whole breath supply was exhausted on the two 'b's', more especially as the glottal aspirate of the terminal 'ch' would make impossible demands upon a depleted arsenal. Hence this

word would become abbreviated to 'B-b-b-barrow', Caper-
caillzie to C-c-caillie, and so on. The final ruse was to abandon
a word altogether if it did not fall to his first burst of fire, and
to substitute another, less difficult. This substitute would often
be wide of the meaning he wanted to convey, and this he
would signify by adding the word 'no' after it and continuing
without losing the impetus of his attack. A comment on the
sporting prospects of his wide but empty moors would thus run
something as follows. 'They tell this year that there are very f-
f-few g-g-g-g-snipe – no – woodcock – no – ph-ph-pheasants –
no – g-g-g-g-*grouse* – *yes*!')

One glance at Aymer and all would have been over; as a
family we suffered from fits of giggles, and this was exactly
the kind of situation that started them, and once started we
were helpless, beyond recall for an unpredictable length of
time. So I concentrated on answering and said: 'We're Aymer
and Gavin Maxwell from Elrig.'

The response was an enthusiastic fusillade. 'I knew your f-f-
father! My name is Jack G-G-G-Gordon.' He rolled his 'R's'
through his nose, if this is possible. 'Are you interested in b-b-
b-*birds*?' Reassured on this vital point, he led us through the
wood to a big grey stone house with an unkempt lawn from
which scores of rabbits scuttled into the rhododendron under-
growth at its sides. We followed him through a fusty hall
where over the chimney-piece was a helmet and breast-plate of
armour and some armorial bearing (it was not until after his
death many years later that we learned that the armour was
wooden), and into a large room where the principal piece of
furniture was a billiard-table. No part of the baize was visible,
for from end to end and from side to side it was covered with
open cardboard boxes where newly arrived rarities nestled in
cotton-wool ('This came today – the Inaccessible M-m-m-
Mountain Thrush'); glass-topped drawers in process of loving
rearrangement; stacks of learned ornithological journals; a
vast variety of implements for drilling and blowing birds' eggs
– the whole clutter of a life-long hobby.

We were wide-eyed. The mysteries that Jack Gordon unfolded to us on that first meeting revised our whole attitude towards the subject, for we had been utterly unaware of the existence of the world-wide cult on whose juvenile fringes we stood, and ignorant of its rules and rituals. We had been brought up never to take more than one, or at most two, eggs from a nest; now we learnt that an egg was valueless and without interest unless it was part of a full set. Eggs stained with droppings we had washed, all unaware that to a real collector these fortuitous excreta were as important as the postmark on a stamp. We had kept a book of notes on our finds, but this did not contain the information required by the high-priests. (It did contain, I see, some fine curiosities; while a shore bird's nest was accurately described as 'a mere scrape in the shingle', a cliff-living sea-bird's eggs were laid, we wrote, in 'a mere scrape in the rock'. Some chicken, some feat.) Jack Gordon showed us what should replace these artless commentaries, printed 'data-cards', headed with 'From the collection of —'; these alone elevated our whole hobby from juvenile to adult status, and soon we were hard at work hammering out the data with my mother's Blick typewriter. (The scrape in the rock somehow got past our proof-reading and survived for posterity.)

Jack Gordon wrote soon after our first meeting, suggesting that we should become junior members of the British Ornithological Union. There was a PS. 'The egg meetings of the BOU are fine.' Dear, kind, lonely, Jack Gordon; he wanted so much more friendship and for so much longer than we could give. However, I think our enthusiasm for his hobby cheered him, and he did not, as one might have predicted, pass into a totally isolated old age; for years later, when his spinal malady finally crippled him, he married his nurse.

All these things that he taught us were fresh offerings for our household gods, the eggs, and the summer holidays that we spent away from Elrig we spent away from every inanimate thing that was dear to us. These places made little impression on me; in fact the year my mother took a flat in Bamburgh Castle, on the Northumberland coast – clear evening skies and

countless swifts racing and wheeling above the tall battle-
ments, the whole air ringing like a balloon glass with their
flight and their voices – is the only summer I remember
well, for although it was August we were able to collect a rich
harvest of rare addled eggs from the Farne Islands.

During the long summer holiday we always had a tutor,
whose function was not so much to teach as to keep us out of
serious mischief. The first of these, Mr Hayter, had just left
Winchester, where he had been captain of the school; but
whatever disciplinarian powers he had shown in that capacity,
he failed hopelessly in face of our particular brand of in-
discipline; our uncontrollable and interminable fits of giggles,
our complex private language of allusion that set them off, our
nauseating habit of using baby talk at home long after we were
schoolboys. Eustace, rebuked by my mother for greed, would
reply in his presence that Mr Hayter had eaten seven bananas,
half a pint of cream and half a pound of sugar after lunch,
which was true and embarrassing for him. A monkey-puzzle
tree we ostentatiously referred to as 'the Hayter tree', and
Eustace, who was going to Winchester, made him apple-pie
beds. As Sir William Hayter, KCMG, British Ambassador to
the USSR from 1953 to 1957, I fancy he must have found life
peaceful by comparison.

Mr Hayter was supplanted by the second master of the
school to which Eustace had gone on leaving Heddon Court.
Richard Curtis was a mountainous young man with a pear-
shaped head, who, despite an easy-going manner of good
humour, was entirely equal to the situation. He had a flying
start by being already in authority over Eustace, and an
occasional cuff from one of those great bear paws (after the
twelfth 'I say, chaps, don't giggle') was as far as he found it
necessary to exert his authority during three years of provocation.

The summer we spent at Bamburgh I was twelve, and had
spent a year at St Wulfric's, halfway through a prison sentence
that ended in escape, however ignominious.

6

UNCONDITIONAL SURRENDER

AT ST WULFRIC'S, I found, like a chicken trying to break out of an eggshell, two perpetual truths – at one moment the sudden chink of light that seemed to lead to a full and untrammelled life, and at the next a chilling wind that made me shrink back into the shell.

A moment of almost mystic exhilaration came from riding. Before I went to school at all I had learned to ride in Richmond Park in the winters; my interest had ended when my pony was chased by a barking bull-terrier and I was bucked off and dragged a hundred yards by one stirrup. At St Wulfric's I took riding as an 'extra'; ponies were brought in pairs by an instructor from the riding school in the town and we rode up on to the big bare sweeps of chalk downs above Beachy Head. My favourite pony was a little bay mare called Giddy, and one shining May morning as I cantered her over the short thymey turf at the summit of the ridge my companion came up abreast of me and urged his pony into a gallop. I did the same, and we were racing neck and neck with the smell of leather and horse and sea wind in my nostrils when I suddenly burst through into a whole world of unsuspected joy and freedom, such a pure ecstasy as a newly fledged eagle might feel in flight. The moment was unique and was never repeated; a week later another pony I was riding lay down and rolled on me in the middle of the Eastbourne traffic, and my enthusiasm did not survive the trauma.

The chill wind blew, too, from the iceberg of Flip's displeasure as she would make her after-luncheon speeches, withering her chosen victims with an unerring though often almost sidelong blast. What rule we were being warned not to infringe again I can't remember, but whatever it was her concluding parenthesis hit me fair and square. 'And that applies equally to young thugs like Scott and desperate nonentities like Maxwell.' Or, 'Matron, I think Maxwell is working that cold of his to death, he can start football again today and cold baths again tomorrow' – and all the admirable robust boys would look at me with contempt and forget that I could shoot and sprint and play quite good cricket.

Because I was as over-sensitive as a hermit crab without a shell these thrusts hurt far more than I believe Flip ever intended them to; she was, I think, basically a kindly person and certainly an extremely efficient one. But she was using her standard technique on very unstandard material, and instead of my being hotted up by St Wulfric's I was slowly reduced to a jelly; in fact the longest period of contentment I can remember there was recovering from measles in the sole company of a Siamese princeling with an enormous and unpronounceable name which had been shortened for practical reasons to Dusdi. Dusdi hated St Wulfric's as much as I did, but for quite different reasons; he had never suffered the least feeling of insufficiency, and viewed the whole school with a sort of noble disdain. He was proficient in some kind of Siamese Ju-jitsu, and he told me he feared no one, either on the staff or among the boys. What he missed, he said, was sex; he explained to me – probably with his tongue far into his brown satin cheek – that he had already been married for some time and that to be forcibly separated from one's wife (or wives, I forget which) was a greater hardship than I could possibly understand. I agreed, and after one brief attempt to explain to me about these unknown joys, he gave up. The subject became mutually taboo, and instead he taught me to write my name in Siamese characters.

Only one other boy at St Wulfric's ever tried to talk to me about sex, and because of my absolute ignorance I put up the barrier of pretended knowledge that insulated me for long afterwards, a barrier so effective by repetition that by the time I had gone on to a public school and my contemporaries were enjoying the sport to the fullness of their rich, simian ingenuity, I was neither better informed nor nearer to pleasure than I had been at birth.

The first conversation arose from my interest in birds (in the dictionary sense). 'So as to lay eggs,' asked my companion, 'do birds have to go through the same process as humans do to have babies?' I was clearly caught right off my guard, so I countered instantly with 'Which process? – there are so many.' 'Are there?' he replied with genuine interest. 'I only know about one.' What he proceeded to describe was utterly unintelligible to me and possibly as wide of the mark as its culmination in birth through the navel, a theory to which I clung long after its improbability should have been apparent. 'Well, as you can imagine,' he concluded, 'it's a very tight fit, and sometimes the baby does get hurt a bit – for instance, those birth-marks on your arm are just where the skin got scraped a little as you came out.' It was that ending that made it impossible to question his theory; at last I had been given a reasonable explanation for the stigmata of which I was so ashamed. It also gave me the opportunity to save my face by saying that of course as birds hadn't got proper navels the whole process was different but it would take too long to explain.

Cyril Connolly's St Wulfric's was full of innocent but intense romance, and, in Flip's eyes, of clandestine experiment; mine was blank, and I aspired neither to friendship nor to love. I saw Heisch once, when he was at his home in the town for a half-term holiday, and on a grey, wintry afternoon we went for a walk along the shingle beaches to a martello tower; all the self-sufficiency of our friendship came back to me with the poignancy of separation, and I cried when I left him, but I found no substitute. Only once and for a moment did a shaft of something half-pleasure and half-pain penetrate me as it had when I saw the painting of the polar bear and the flaming Arctic night in Matron's room at Heddon Court. Robina's favourite playmate was a boy named Vivian, a vivacious and beautiful ash-blond with such a fine soprano voice that he sang in distant cathedral choirs. With him, and sometimes with me, by invitation, she broke such school rules as she dared, exploring the vast rubbish dump behind the chapel (a tangled mass of rusty iron in which treasure was constantly and confidently expected), raiding the larder, smoking her mother's cigarettes, or climbing about the roofs and the fire-escapes at night. It was on one of these last escapades, with moon and stars bright beyond the darkness of the tall chimneys, that Robina dared Vivian to sing. He sang, first *Heilige Nacht*, quite softly but with intense emotion, then *Adeste Fideles*, beginning almost muted, but slowly allowing the full volume of his voice to take over the first refrain so that it soared wild and high and infinitely pure into the brilliant sky, and my throat contracted as if I wanted to cry.

Other boys in general made very little impression on me; I was too scared of the wood to examine many of the trees or in much detail. Sometimes an act of generosity or especial hostility forced one of them upon my notice, and a senior boy who succeeded momentarily in making me feel genuinely ashamed of myself remains as an image utterly unfogged by time. My mother had sent me a small leather-bound portable inkwell. During prep, the first evening of my ownership of it, I placed it on my desk and used it and its purple ink instead of the sunk china inkwell that held a marshy mixture of blotting-paper and Stephen's blue-black. A senior boy named Bird was supervising prep, and as he patrolled the desks he noticed my inkwell and forbade me to use it, adding as a rider, 'You've got to learn to be like other people.' This seemed to me unfair, more especially as I had asked my mother for this object in preference to a fountain-pen, and the next day I took it to Flip and asked her ingenuously whether, since it had been sent to me as a present, I might use it. She assented instantly, and even condescended to admire it. Bird did not see it again for several days, and during that time the whole school knew that he had received news of his father's death. I had no idea that it was he who had been detailed as warden when I was given a hundred lines to write out for something or other that I had done; I went into the empty classroom, put the inkwell in front of me, and began to write my lines. After a few minutes he came in, and without glancing at me, walked across the room and stood staring out of the window. I thought of putting the inkwell into the desk, but realized that it would only make enough noise to attract his attention to me. I went on writing my lines, hoping that he was going to ignore me altogether. But after a while he turned and walked slowly down the room, and when he was close to me I looked up and saw that he had been crying. His very light bright blue eyes (even to the hair he was exactly like Jackie Coogan at the same age) were reddened and full of tears, and when he spoke his voice was husky and strained. 'I thought I told you you couldn't use that thing, Maxwell.' I had absolutely no feeling of triumph or of spite, only of defence, as I replied: 'I asked Mrs Brunt, and she said I could.'

Bird stood looking down at me for what seemed a long time without speaking; then he said: 'I see. That gives me a very clear insight into your character, Maxwell. I hope you're feeling very proud of your little score.' He turned and went back to the window, and never looked round again while I was in the room. When I had done the lines I said: 'I've finished – may I go now, Bird?' He just said 'Yes' in a flat voice. Then I said, because it was true, 'I'm sorry about the ink, Bird,' but he didn't answer, so I had to go. I went to the lavatory and sat there wondering what his father had been like, and where they had lived, and what sort of pictures were passing in front of Bird's mental eye as he stared out of the window for all that time. His father I pictured as a big man, ash-blond like Bird, and with the same bright blue eyes, and he was happy and carefree. For some reason I decided that they lived on the coast, probably in Devon or Cornwall, and that Bird and his father sailed small yachts together and had campfire meals on small, remote islands. After a time I was almost in tears myself.

If there was a precise point during that second year at St Wulfric's when my dull unhappiness turned to active misery it was the recurrence of night horrors that had made their appearance a few years earlier and which I believed I had outgrown. They had never been frequent, but they were of such dreadful intensity that each was like a death in itself. There is no word adequate to describe the terror that I experienced during those dreams; there were two, always recurrent down to the minutest detail, utterly unlike each other and yet equal in their appalling impact. Thinking of them now I can almost feel again a strange dusty contraction of the throat that accompanied them, and that I did not guess until after that time at St Wulfric's was due to screaming, for I had never before been told how I behaved during my sojourns in that other world.

In the first of these dreams I was playing on the lawn at Tynewood with my sister; the house was behind us, and beyond the lawn was woodland, fringed with rhododendrons. It was a strange half-light, the kind of darkness at noon that may come with a freak thunderstorm or an eclipse of the sun. There were many daisies on the lawn, and I was holding one in my hand when something like the mouth of a gigantic cannon, a vast, gaping circle of darkness, ringed with dull metal, loomed out of the trees and grew until there was room for nothing else but it. There was no action, no attempt on my part to escape, only the object itself and the ultimate extreme of fear.

In the second dream the whole of my vision was filled by a ceiling, an ordinary undecorated ceiling of a pale grey colour. On the surface of this, at the far left and close to the corner, was an object that never came into absolute focus; it appeared to be a short, dark leather strap like a dog collar. Nothing moved; as in the other dream, terror was in the object itself.

Which of the two returned to shatter me at St Wulfric's I don't remember. I regained consciousness sitting up in bed, still screaming, with Flip and the Matron and the Matron's assistant, all in their dressing-gowns, holding on to me and trying to quieten me, while the rest of the boys in the dormitory stood in a scared huddle near the door. They told me

'We habitually wore kilts of black and white shepherd's plaid'

Elrig: North side

Elrig: South side

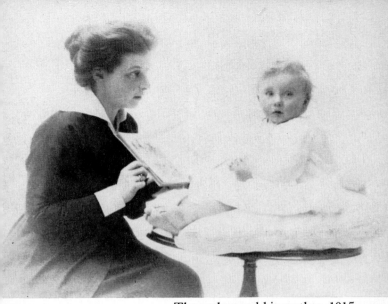

The author and his mother, 1915

The Maxwell children, 1917

Gavin and Christian Maxwell

Aymer with Andrew the Owl

With the Jackdaw

With Christian and Carlo . . .

. . . and with a lamb

Judy

Bob Hannam

Christian, Eustace, Alftruda the goat, Aymer and Carlo

Aymer, Gavin and the heron, 1928

afterwards that I had never stopped screaming at the full pitch of my lungs for a whole quarter of an hour.

It is easy to confuse cause and effect. It may be that my increasing unhappiness and insecurity at St Wulfric's produced these symptoms, or perhaps the public shame that I felt after them deepened my misery and loneliness as I believe it did. Probably I exaggerated in my mind the importance of the exhibition to other boys who knew of it; looking back now it seems that we were tolerant enough among ourselves of the oddities in the school, the bed-wetters and sleep-walkers, and even of one boy who came to the school while I was there and whom Flip, in one of her after-luncheon talks, had told us all to be kind to because his mind had never developed since he was three. (Whatever action he performed he would seek reassurance, turning anxiously to the nearest person and asking: 'Styles good boy?' Once he showed me a postcard from his mother, and I wondered what he made of it, for it was written in polysyllabic English as from one adult to another.)

Whichever was cause and whichever effect, the end result of my nightmare was the same – I couldn't bear St Wulfric's any longer. I gave up even trying to produce work acceptable to the masters or behaviour acceptable to the boys, and I viewed the least punishment as persecution, the least sadistic ragging as bullying. I was determined to be removed from the school, but I realized that because of my snob value I would have to do something very dreadful indeed to be sacked from it. So, instead, I wrote to my mother telling her that I was miserable and asking if I could go somewhere else next term. Because of Flip's unofficial system of censorship I couldn't post this letter in the ordinary way, so using the route of roof and fire-escape that I knew so well from moonlight escapades with Robina and Vivian, I climbed out in dressing-gown and pyjamas and posted it in a pillar-box on the road beyond the drive gates. Whether I was by this time under some sort of surveillance or whether it was chance, I was caught on the way back, and under a puzzled gruelling from Flip I refused to say what I had been doing. I realize now that because I had been alone

105

her mind was exploring all possibilities from the most perilous type of secret assignation to plain madness – possibilities that must have caused her great alarm. Thousands of boys had passed through her shrewd and capable hands, and she had probably swerved round most types of scandal with the same impatient skill as she manoeuvred her Willys Knight through the Eastbourne traffic; it must have been plain to her that she was going to have to swerve again, but the other vehicle was giving no signals at all. I emerged from the interview tear-stained but intact, apart from one of those automatic lies with which children reply to leading questions if they have not yet lost their tempers. 'You're happy here, aren't you?' she had wheedled, putting a motherly arm around my shoulder – brown silk bosom with a faint blend of expensive scent and tobacco – and I had snivelled, 'Yes, Mum,' when she drew my head against her breast.

Even the small victory of having posted the letter undetected intensified the siege in my mind, both because of this lie which was outside my rules of war, and because I overheard a group of boys talking about the real reason for my outing. Obviously, they said, it was connected with my screaming fit in the night – I had been sleep-walking. The injustice of this was more than I could take, and I went for the speaker like a wildcat – my first really aggressive action since I had used to fight Studley at Heddon Court. The result was inconclusive, but left enough visible evidence to lead to both of us being hauled before Flip. I couldn't deny that I had been the attacker, and because I again refused to say why – not for any tactical reason but because shame prevented me repeating the slander – I was punished, mildly. I was kept in my classroom during free time and made to write out some slogan about good behaviour. I was not supervised all the time, and I used part of it to write a thoroughly hysterical letter to my mother, which ended, 'For God's sake take me away from this awful place.' That night I climbed out again, by a different route, and posted my letter in a different pillar-box on the other side of the playing-fields. This time nobody saw me.

My mother responded, thinking that there must be something badly wrong for such a normally manageable child to call the full orchestra, and as she was unable to come herself she sent my Aunt Victoria to take me away. Flip told me that she was coming and that my clothes were already packed; faced now with a *fait accompli* she was sweet and kind and clearly actuated by a deep personal curiosity. She still had no idea what it was all about; in fact I was the only person who had and it just wouldn't go into words. I waited for my aunt in Flip's sitting-room, with Flip for company, and instead of feeling triumph I felt something akin to remorse. On analysis it was, I think, a form of self-pity for failure to make a success of anything, for not understanding why I had failed, and having blamed Flip for so much that at this particular moment seemed trivial.

Flip on her side, was determined to classify the matter under one of her systematic labels, and time was short. It was not until I could actually hear my aunt's car on the drive that she reverted to the unreliable technique of leading questions. She put her arm round me again and said with deep sympathy, 'You've been bullied, haven't you.' It was a statement, not a question, and it seemed an excellent way out of my difficulties, so I nodded dumbly. Then the front doorbell rang and she said: 'We'll have to say goodbye in a few minutes. It was Stott, wasn't it.' Again it was a statement, and again, despicably, I nodded. Stott was an overgrown lout of nearly fourteen; he was generally aggressive and unpleasant to smaller boys, but he had never picked on me in particular. Satisfied that everything was now cleared up, that her investigations had at the eleventh hour yielded the underlying facts of the case, Flip became briskly friendly. 'You should have told me. He'll be leaving at the end of the next term anyway, but now here's your aunt.'

Damp goodbyes – Flip had tears in her eyes, though from what emotion I find it hard to guess – and my aunt and I had hardly driven a mile from the school before I wanted to go back and tell Flip that it wasn't Stott at all and that everything was my fault. But it was too late to do anything.

I left St Wulfric's in the middle of the spring term, a few months before my thirteenth birthday, and went straight to Elrig. There in the cold bright March weather, with the rooks already building in the elms and all the sights and scents and sounds of home about me, I eliminated St Wulfric's from my conscious mind, allowing entry only to Mr Sillar when he sent me his collection of bird skins. The rest of the term, before my brothers came back from school, Aymer from Eton and Eustace from Winchester, I spent as I had been used to after they had first gone to school and I was still at home; long days with Hannam the gamekeeper as he went the rounds of his distant traps, close at his heels as a shadow while with the wisdom of a lifetime he outwitted birds and beasts classified by his rules as vermin, listening to the low rumble of his voice as, sheltering behind a stone dyke from some blinding hill shower, he would try to impart to me his intimate knowledge of wild life. At the end of some long speech or reminiscence he would pause, tamp the black tobacco dottle in his pipe, and add, 'Ay, you come to know, through time.'

Hannam, dead twenty years now; still looking a man in his prime when alone among his traps in a tumbled spinney he found himself lying helpless, paralysed, reduced from the dictator of the woods to a pitiful human without power to rise from the ground. All my life I had taken Hannam so much for granted that there was no possible reassessment at his death; though it was simultaneous with the extinction of so many other valued lives, he took with him the greater part of my childhood.

Hannam had come to Elrig in 1922, and he lived in a lonely cottage on the shore of Elrig Loch. Peat-smoke and pale evening skies reflected in the water; a slow, rumbling voice containing a concealed, absolute command. He was of medium height, individual both in feature and in figure. To the end of his life his hair was wavy and raven-black; his eyes were blue, and his large and usually ragged moustache was foxy red. His torso, I remember from watching him cutting peats under a summer sun, was white-skinned and hairless. More usually it was clad in a rough and ancient suit of tweeds, ending in great boat-shaped dubbined boots below baggy plus-fours. The tweeds smelled of dog, stoat, mole, black tobacco and human sweat, with an undertone of peat-smoke and bog myrtle. His accent, due to Yorkshire birth and long residence in Galloway, was a most curious compound; heavily stressed h's preceded every initial vowel, and I can't have been more than eight or so when we compounded a sentence born of Hannam's rowing instruction on Elrig Loch, and his continual imparting of natural lore. 'The howl wouldn't sit on the hoars and heat the heggs in the hevening.'

Hannam had come from the great grouse-moors of Yorkshire in their Edwardian hey-day when the existence of a moor and a manor meant the livelihood of hundreds of people; he had watched Lord Ripon ('Lord de Grey, as he would have been then') kill his sixty brace of grouse in a single drive; had loaded for Lord Walsingham and Sir Ralph Payne-Galway, and all the other hyphenated play-boys of the time. They were, to him, criticizable in limited terms; they shot well or they shot badly; they were, at the end of the day, generous or mean, friendly or Olympic; but no matter how they behaved they remained his gods.

'It was skill they aimed at, just skill. I've seen me loading to Lord Ripon – Lord de Grey as he would have been then – and we were waiting at a covert side for the pheasants to come. It was blackbirds that came first, high and almost out of range and being blown about by the wind. He downed every one of them, and fired a hundred cartridges before the first pheasant came. He was just keeping his hand in.' Hannam saw nothing strange, nothing reprehensible in this cool destruction to further the aims of pure skill; his extremely able intellect operated within the perimeter of his own profession, and in this and his surprising hobbies he, too, aimed at pure skill. By instinct he was an engineer, and close to the kennels he had built himself a workshop, made from hammered-out oil-drums and containing lathes and drills beyond the comprehension of a child. He could make anything and he could mend anything, and in all he attempted he was content with no less than perfection. For all close work he wore a pair of quite circular steel-rimmed spectacles which magnified enormously, and through these he would watch, as though impersonally, his huge horny hands trying to enclose between finger and thumb some tiny screw or washer. Elrig depended on him in innumerable ways; to mend the clocks and any other mechanical thing that might be broken, and beyond these more specialized functions he would cut the winter's peat-stack, sweep the chimneys, and with a pony and trap make a weekly visit to Kirkcowan Station eleven miles distant across the moors. In conversation he was always stimulating, introducing into his anecdotes a wealth of lore wrapped in piquantly individual phraseology. Introducing a thought, for example; 'Lying in my bed with my feet at a quarter to three, I said to myself . . .', or, recounting a shooting anecdote: 'Well, then, someone went up the hill to look; let me see, would it be Lord Ripon? Na, na. Would it be Lord Walsingham? Na, I dinna think so. Would it be myself? I believe it would. Yes, it would be myself.'

At that age I still hated to see anything killed, and the sight of one of his great boat-shaped boots crushing a curled-up hedgehog newly released from a gin-trap; of a stoat that in its efforts to break free had almost chewed through one of its forelegs, only to be killed now by a blow from Hannam's stick; of a magpie not quite dead from strychnine poisoning sucked from a doctored hen's egg; all these things produced in me a revulsion that for the time being survived Hannam's rationalizations. 'They all come to die,' he would say, 'there's no mercy in nature, and like as not their natural deaths'd be worse'n that. The stoat eats the rabbit alive, screaming away for twenty minutes or more, and he'll kill maybe a thousand rabbits in his lifetime. And if a hawk (he pronounced it 'hark') can get its feet on a young stoat he's not bothering whether his claws go in the guts or the heart or whether the beast's dead when he starts eating. Na, na. A man doesn't like to see suffering, but it's there whether he looks at it or not.' I tried to take in the truths of Hannam's philosophies – they extended far beyond animals and pain, into the realms of courage, courtesy, philosophy and religion. He had no use for churches or ministers. One day the minister of Mochrum chid him for his perennial absence from the pews, and Hannam explained that if a gamekeeper went to church poachers took his place in the woods. The minister was not satisfied and began a tirade, but Hannam cut him short. 'Na, na, Minister, we're the Dodos, and we maunna fall out wi' each other – the next generation will have nae use for your profession or for mine.'

Despite Hannam's insistence on the absolutely ephemeral nature of all life, try as I would I still identified myself with every animal in suffering or the act of death. But now I kept this weakness, which I equated with my failures in conformity at school, concealed from all but Hannam, and when my sister asked him what happened to a magpie that had eaten strychnine I had acquired enough bravado to guffaw at the exchange that followed. Hannam looked at her very solemnly and answered: 'They sneeze and they sneeze and they sneeze until their heads fly off, Miss Christian.' 'Oh, *Hannam*!' said my sister, all the world's compassion in her voice. 'How *horrible*!'

My brothers came home from school and at once Aymer and I were again immersed in 'the collection', the perilous climbing of an infinite variety of trees – eye-sticking firs where every one of a thousand green-dusted branches and twigs were rotten; budding elms branchless for many feet, and ending in swaying tops above which rooks wheeled giddily against a tilted sky; the thorny, tweed-tearing grip of hawthorn trees with the basket of a magpie's nest at the top; the raw red bark of a great Scots pine into which the bite of the shoe-strapped climbing-irons was as satisfying as the crunch of a biscuit; the slow, cautious, often terrifying descent carrying the plundered eggs in the peak of a tweed cap. Sometimes my brother would say, as might some famous Himalayan mountaineer, 'I can't climb today,' and add, 'something on the ground or shrub stuff, thrushes and blackbirds,' and then it was brambles, or the infinitely denser and more prickly *Berberis darwinii* or the needles of unthinned sitka no more than eight feet high. Whatever it was, and no matter how much blood was drawn, it was home.

7

TO LEARN TO THINK

MY MOTHER, having taken her decision to remove me from St Wulfric's, behaved with an exemplary restraint. She never grilled me about what had gone wrong, put no leading questions and helped me to think of it as a chapter that was over; in fact she hardly alluded to the subject at all until, in the early days of those Easter holidays, she told me where I was going next, and this she did with an impeccable grace and tact. She asked me whether I liked Mr Curtis, who had been our tutor during two years' holidays and I said truthfully that I did. She told me that as I had now been to two schools I must really make a success of the third; that Eustace had been happy at Hurst Court, that Mr Curtis was second master there and that there would be a friendly climate from the start. I think I did say that I never wanted to go to school again and couldn't I stay at home, but the conversation on her side was so rational that the phase was almost momentary, and I accepted that I was going to Hurst Court at the beginning of the summer term. I asked Eustace what it was like, and he was informative as always. A short series of character-sketches and admonitions and an atmosphere of 'just mention my name' and I felt completely reassured. At the end of the holidays I arrived with my mother at Hurst Court in our odd open Studebaker, driven by the least eccentric chauffeur in the series, and for the first time I ended a holiday without shedding a tear.

Everything in this partially contrived, partially fortuitous situation was in my favour. Contrived because the staff of the school took me on with the full knowledge that I was 'difficult', if not hopeless, and because my mother had with a sort of *tour de force* born of faith persuaded me that this simply must be a success; fortuitous because I came at the beginning of a summer term, when my liking for cricket and running were active assets and my hatred of football was not yet apparent; fortuitous, or midway between that and contrived, that I could bask in the afterglow of Eustace's sunshine. Bouncing, extrovert, aggressive and friendly, Eustace had left a solid, bulbous reputation behind him; he had not only come up to standard in every way but had been one of the most distinguished wicket-keepers in the school's history. As his brother, and as one of a dozen boys among sixty who were at or about thirteen years of age, I commanded an automatic respect that could be lessened only by overt failure in the schoolboy sense, the sense of something incomprehensible that must be destroyed. Eustace was the bridge; because he had been accepted I was acceptable, and with this knowledge, soon sensed, I blossomed into a secondhand security.

The day after I arrived I was subjected to an interview by the headmaster. In my mind all headmasters' studies were filled with dense blue pipe-smoke, and Dr Vaughan-Evans's was no exception, but in this case my whole attention was focused upon the man rather than upon the uncongenial atmosphere. He was something quite new to me, and the small information that I had about him only added to his obvious stature. I knew that he had been a pilot in the Royal Flying Corps during the First World War and that he had been decorated for bravery. I knew that he was a Doctor of Philosophy; I knew that he was a man supposedly subject to 'moods', and in any case was not to be trifled with. The image that this intelligence had formed was nebulous, but entirely contrary to the presence confronting me.

Dr Vaughan-Evans was a short man, five foot nine at most and though not fat he had a small, neat pot-belly. He wore dark, formal single-breasted suits, with a stand-up hard collar and broad-knotted tie and highly polished black ankle-boots. Below the chin the whole image was totally misleading; to integrate the power of his head with that pompous little body was something that only a schoolboy, with his elastic ability to accept any authority, could possibly contrive. The head was in no way out of proportion except in emphasis, in impact, but it belonged to an entirely different body. Sallow, saturnine, cynical, huge grey eyes under a balding dome that had been black, he was as capable of looking right through a boy by pure abstraction as by pure concentration. We had bets as to who could stare out V.-E. but no boy ever won. His voice belonged to the head rather than to the body, strong and harsh but with an unusually perfect diction.

When I came into the room he was standing with his back to the fire, puffing at his pipe, legs apart and his weight resting characteristically upon the balls of his feet. He said: 'Sit down,' and I perched nervously on the extreme edge of a big leather armchair. What he said was so short and to the point that I remember nearly every word of it.

'Well, Gavin, you're at Hurst Court now, and you've got four terms here before you go to a public school. While you're here things are going to go right – and it's up to you first and me second to see that they do. All you've got to do is your best, nothing less and nothing different – that's what I expect from you, and as long as I think you're doing it we shall be friends. Try to get on with the other boys, concentrate on what you have in common with them and put aside the things that are different. There are no ogres at Hurst Court, masters or boys, and everyone's prepared to like you. One thing you've got is decent manners – keep them, whether you're talking to a boy of eight or the headmaster.' During all this speech his eyes never left mine, and he never blinked. Then, after a short pause, he said: 'You come from a powerful family – your uncle's President of the Board of Education besides being our local MP here. That means nothing to me where you're concerned; it's as a boy at Hurst Court that you succeed or fail, and if I were you I should make up my mind to succeed, and no buts or doubts. That's all. Good luck.'

Because, I suppose, this was a period of anxiety for my mother, she kept the letters that I wrote to her during my first term; looking at them now it is difficult to believe that the handwriting is that of a boy not yet thirteen, and a timid insecure one at that. The content, too, exudes confidence and a general zest for life. By the first of them I had already been made captain of the second cricket eleven. 'Of course it is an absolutely different system of things from St Wulfric's or Heddon Court, and it is rather confusing at first; but I think I shall like it very much.' I wrote for my stamp collection (we had not been allowed them at St Wulfric's) and for pictures of birds to decorate my cubicle; by the second I had run my fastest hundred yards yet, and got in a family jibe about my brother Eustace's weight: 'I can't really imagine Doody coming in 2nd in the high jump, can you? That apparently is what he did here last year!' The extreme normality of these letters must have been reassuring to my mother after the storms of St Wulfric's, as must have been my request to 'please choose livestock of some sort' for a birthday-present, 'or if not something that would in some way be useful for "the eggs"'.

After I had been at Hurst Court for a week, Dr Vaughan-Evans wrote to my mother:

'Dear Lady Mary,

'Gavin has settled down quite satisfactorily; he appears perfectly normal in every way. I do not know what he will say to you in his letter tomorrow, but he seems quite happy and cheery. His work is satisfactory and he has started at the nets and first game in cricket. I have great hopes of him becoming a fast bowler, but he won't get into the first eleven this year I think.

'You will give me some idea of what he says in his letter to you, won't you? But my honest opinion is that from all points of view the position is most satisfactory. I do hope that a load has really been lifted from your mind.

'With our kind regards,
'Yours sincerely,
'H. B. Vaughan-Evans.'

On Sunday mornings we all trooped to a small local church, where Dr Vaughan-Evans preached the sermon himself. His first sermon took me absolutely aback. 'Religion is a thing of reason and not of emotion,' he announced in his clear, harsh voice. 'We must beware of any sort of feeling of uplift – such as you may experience when hearing or singing a beautiful hymn – and try to avoid it at all cost. Religion is a set of rules by which we live, and in a state of emotional uplift we can no more hope to keep a set of rules than a drunk man can walk in a straight line. The actions of a man under the influence of alcohol can be compared to those of a man under the influence of emotion.' I thought of the hymn 'Far, far away like bells at evening pealing' that used to fetch tears to my eyes at Heddon Court, and of Vivian singing *Adeste Fideles* on the moonlit rooftops of St Wulfric's, and felt sad that my source of beauty was suspect.

But my sadness did not last, for the pleasantness of Hurst Court was almost bewildering. From the start I found myself treated with deference by all boys younger than I; with the elixir of open friendliness by my contemporaries; with kindness and patience by the staff. Dr V.-E., who had detected a streak of precocity that he found piquant, played a game with me from which he derived pleasure and I profit. The exchanges usually took place at meals, and most often at breakfast. He sat at the head of the first table – there were three – and the eldest boys occupied the first few places on either side of him. While we ate our bread and margarine he ended his meal with huge quantities of toast and chunky marmalade; and, as he munched, his large abstracted eyes would suddenly meet mine. When his mouth was next empty he would say with startling abruptness, 'Are you better?' My new-found popularity was at stake and my peers in audience; I could not let the challenge go by. 'Better than what, sir?' 'Better than you were.' Pause on my side; no one but Uncle Willie had ever used words as a ruthless game, and it was something to be learned, something that I felt I could learn. 'I haven't been ill, sir.' 'I didn't ask whether you had been ill; I asked whether you were better. Are you better?'

Once I tried saying 'No, sir', almost giggling with the spirit of the game, while a barrister's sadistic half-smile took over half his face. 'You're not better? I'm very sorry about that; I'd hoped you would be. Do you expect to get better?' To this I tried both yes and no; to the first he replied: 'In that case it's clearly my duty as your headmaster, and in common courtesy, to inquire every morning whether your hope has been fulfilled,' and to the second: 'Then I suppose you must resign yourself to being as you are. How are you?' Automatically, 'Very well, thank you sir.' 'I'm very glad indeed to hear that. But I fail to understand how it equates with your pessimistic attitude of a moment ago,' and pushing back his chair noisily, darting a conspiratorial look of triumph, he would exit, black and bouncing.

He would vary this game as opportunity arose. Finding me during free time engaged on an ambitious water-colour painting of a Great Black-backed Gull he looked over my shoulder and said: 'What is that?' 'A gull, sir.' 'You think you gull mother, don't you? What's it doing?' 'Dying, sir.' (The concept had been inspired by seeing a Great Black-backed Gull shot by Hannam with the mystery of a cut cartridge, as it rested upon a rock seemingly two gunshots away.) 'Well, if the gull is dying, perhaps it means you won't try to gull your mother any more. Let me know when it is dead.'

Sometimes he was very disconcerting. Having expounded to the whole school one day the principle of the aneroid barometer, he asked whether there were any questions. In absolute innocence and with a genuine desire to understand more, I put up my hand and said: 'Sir, we've got one which is like two drums of paper in a glass case, and an arm with ink on it traces a line on the paper when the glass is going up and down.' Something in his expression warned me of uncomprehended danger, and I stopped. He stared at me in complete silence for something like half a minute, as usual without blinking, and then said harshly: 'Then you're very lucky. Has anyone else got a question?' Slowly, I realized that he thought I had been

118

trying to impress, to boast, that I was flying in the face of his warning to concentrate on the things I had in common with other boys and to put aside the rest. I had not had the least idea that barographs were more expensive than other kinds of barometer; now I guessed it and turned scarlet as every boy in the school stared at me, wondering what I had done wrong.

This was one of a very few incidents that marred a contented year under his charge. Each was based upon misunderstanding, and each I can remember with the greatest clarity. During my second term at Hurst Court the head boy of the school and I decided to produce a school magazine of our own. It revolved, I remember, round my own interest in animals and birds, and a newly acquired enthusiasm for racing-cars, for I had recently seen Sir Henry Birkin lap Brooklands at something like 140 mph. It was illustrated by photographs and drawings, and was called *The Overall*, a title intended to convey supremacy rather than industry, and its first number carried an introductory ditty by the cleverest of the masters. '*The Overall* is over all, and so for all you know, it might amuse you to peruse the latest news below.' This seemed to us the epitome of urbane wit. 'Articles and stories by all the masters!' our cover announced in flaring red letters. 'More than sixty pages packed with interest!' We had received official sanction for this project from Dr Vaughan-Evans, and on Sunday morning after church we were to present it to him. He sat at the rostrum, and we made a formal ceremony of it, walking up the aisle between the rows of desks, each holding one side of the first and only number of *The Overall*. 'So this is the pinafore, is it,' he said heartily. 'May I keep it for half an hour?' He did, and returned it with some kindly comments; probably he was pleasantly surprised to find so many of his staff to be literate.

There was not intended to be anything clandestine about our charging a halfpenny to read our magazine; if at that charge it had been read by every boy in the school we should have earned half a crown, certainly less than our production costs in photographs and paper. It was in brisk circulation that evening, and had been read by some twenty boys, when Dr Vaughan-Evans entered the big classroom at the exact moment when a halfpenny was changing hands. He bore down upon us like an avenging angel, his eyes grim and his voice mighty with wrath. *The Overall* was confiscated, and we were told to visit him separately in his study before we went to bed. The subsequent tirade seemed to me out of all proportion to the gravity of the offence; he could hardly have been angrier or more outraged if we had been caught trying to blow up the school buildings with dynamite. He ended with: 'If there's any repetition of this or any other kind of trouble I shall have to say that you're unsatisfactory, and you know what *that* means.' The trouble was that I didn't – it was one of those terrifying words that gave a desperate feeling of insecurity but had no precise meaning at all. But it had enough impact to kill *The Overall* stone dead within twenty-four hours of its birth.

The next occasion was a misunderstanding too. I had made a close friend of a boy a little younger than myself, a highly engaging and witty urchin called Craith – by definition a faun – whose parents lived in South America and who was being brought up by a maiden aunt on the outskirts of Hastings. I used to go with him to this house on Sunday afternoons sometimes, and we would go through his collection of birds' eggs or play table-tennis or stump cricket in the garden. His aunt, for some reason, was seldom there. On the day in question we arrived back to find that the whole school had gone into tea, and as we had a further hour of official freedom we decided just to wander about and amuse ourselves. Round at the back of the buildings, close to the school lavatories, we put up a tin can on the top of a wall about twenty yards away and started trying to hit it with pebbles. We became completely absorbed in the sport, and nearly half an hour passed before we heard the unmistakable footsteps of Dr Vaughan-Evans approaching. (His boots creaked.) By common instinct we scuttled for the adjoining lavatories and each locked ourselves into a compartment. The footsteps creaked directly into the building and the headmaster's voice, harsh with authority, demanded: 'Who's there?' Each of us waited for the other to reply, and after some seconds he said again: 'I asked, who is there?' This time I replied: 'Maxwell, sir.' 'And?' The voice was definitely menacing. 'Craith, sir.'

There was a brief pause. Then, 'Maxwell, come to my study immediately you leave the lavatory. Craith, I will send for you later.' We heard him turn and walk away and his footsteps grew faint down the passage. We consulted hurriedly in whispers. 'Say we were throwing bits of earth – it sounds better than stones,' said Craith. I hurried to the headmaster's study and knocked timidly. He had his back to me, lighting his pipe, and said 'Sit down' without turning round. When he did so he said: 'Tell me what you've been doing all day.' I tried to remember, and told him truthfully everything we'd done until we left Craith's house. He interrupted then to ask whether Craith's aunt had been there, and I replied that she had not. 'And then, after you'd got back, which must have been more than half an hour ago, what did you do then?'

'We were throwing pieces of earth at a tin can, sir.'

'Was that all?'

'Yes, sir.'

'Then why were you in the lavatory?'

Seeing me hesitate, he substituted another question. 'How well do you know Craith?'

'Pretty well, sir.'

Dr Vaughan-Evans impaled me with his huge hypnotic eyes.

'It is possible that you don't know him as well as I do. It is also possible that you know him even better, which I should not like to think. In your own interests I am going to tell you something about Craith which may not be news to you. I am not inquiring whether it is or is not. Craith is a fine boy in many ways, and he has what people call charm, but he has a dirty mind, and he has come near to being expelled from this school more than once. It is possible that I should have expelled him if his parents did not live abroad. That is why I sent for you when I found you alone in the lavatories with him. Do you understand?'

I didn't, except that some unknown, forbidden subject was in the air, something of which I was afraid. I blushed deeply and said nothing.

'You may go now. Send me Craith.'

Craith came out from his interview in tears. 'He told me what he'd said to you about me. But it's not true – it used to be, but it's not true now. But he's warned you against me. Does this mean we part company?'

I'd already made up my mind about this. 'No. Even V.-E. didn't ask me to. As far as I'm concerned I'm going to forget all about it.' With a sudden harsh little sob he leaned forward and kissed me on the cheek, then he ran away. Neither of us ever spoke directly of it again, nor, surprisingly, was there any feeling of restraint on either side; but I think there was trauma to both of us. Poor precocious, charming Craith, all that nature intended him to be condemned as dirty, unacceptable, dangerous, contaminating, his physical beauty by itself suspect. In receiving that one sexless kiss for expiation I had no feeling of magnanimity; I only knew that he was ashamed of something, and that I didn't want to be an ally of his enemies. Human acts of faith are rare; somehow we had momentarily achieved one, and each had gained stature.

Later, Craith said: 'You know when one's grown up things are going to be much more difficult. Everybody *wants* something from one, as far as I can see. Well, I *want* too, and I'm going to get what I want. In ten years' time you'll see.' I never saw him after I left Hurst Court; perhaps he is still alive (for Pan I pray not) but I have been told that he was killed flying a Spitfire in the Battle of Britain. I would prefer to think so, for given his background and his multiple interviews with the headmaster there can have been no likely third possibility beyond heroic death or dishonour in a hypocritical world; perhaps having accepted the second he defied the first, and like many others erased himself in a reeling holocaust of fire and pain, too late to kiss an ally's cheek as he had kissed mine.

Like Mr Stallard at Heddon Court, Dr Vaughan-Evans had a standard question which was put to every boy in the school at some stage in his career, but the difference in the question emphasized the different poles of personality at which the two headmasters stood. Whereas Mr Stallard's question had concerned the finding of a lost cricket-ball, a practical problem that might, one felt, continue to concern him for the rest of his days, Dr Vaughan-Evans was typically concerned with intellectual education and more especially with the development of a critical faculty. He would enter the classroom, bouncing on creaking black boots, his Doctor of Philosophy's gown already billowing slightly as if impatient to unburden itself of wisdom, and the master who was teaching would move respectfully to one side of the rostrum and fall silent. Planting himself squarely behind the desk, wrapping his restless gown about him and rocking slowly up and down on the balls of his feet, the headmaster would send his hypnotic eyes to probe those of each of the dozen or so pupils before him. When he spoke it was with a harshness that invariably led the class to imagine him about to announce the discovery of some unthinkable crime among their number.

'I have a question to ask you. I shall ask each of you in turn.' Pause. (At this point more than one boy would begin to blush or show other signs of nervousness and distress.) 'If when I leave this room anyone of you does not know or fully understand the answer, there will be little point in your remaining at this school.' ('Golly!' breathed Craith on my left, 'he's going to sack someone!') 'The question I am going to put to you is simple, but you must think before replying. It is: what did you come to this school for? I want no facetious answers such as that your parents sent you here – you must interpret the question as being "What is the purpose in this stage of your education?" I trust I have made myself perfectly plain.' (On my left I just hear Craith articulate: 'As the Duchess said, removing her wig.' He had a joke, or tears, for everything.)

'Prior?'

'To – er – to learn, sir.'

'Learn what?'

'Well, whatever we're taught, sir.'

'Ashton?'

'To learn to earn a living when we're grown up, sir.'

'Pratt?'

'To pass Common Entrance exam, sir.'

The headmaster's gaze lingered a moment on Pratt's Humboldt-Woolly-Monkey-face. 'You are not a fool, Pratt. That is *an* aim, but a subsidiary aim.'

One after another we all tried to be cleverer than the others, but none of us gave the answer he required.

'As far as I am concerned,' he announced, using all the hard cutting quality of his personality in voice and eyes, 'you came here for one purpose only – you came here to *learn* to *think*. Now, it is not enough to remember that answer and trot it out to please me or anyone else. You must understand what it means. It means you must use your brains on everything you're ever told or asked. Test the truth of your own statements and other people's by applying your *brains* to them. This the only way in which man moves forward.' Pause. 'This does not mean that if you use your brains on a school rule and find it to be a silly rule you may break it. It does mean that you may say "I have thought about this or that school rule, I have used my *brains* on it, and I think it is a silly rule but while I am here I must keep it." As a matter of fact, we have no rules here that are silly, and if you think you find one I shall be glad to explain why it exists. I used my brains in making the rules – I didn't just pull them out of a hat. I have learned to think, and you have come here to do the same. Please resume mathematics, Mr Glover.'

But Mr Glover, or Mr Chivers, or Mr Hall rarely did – the rest of the classroom period was spent, willy-nilly, on discussing the meaning of thought.

8

CIPHERS WITHOUT CODE

DURING THE year that I was at Hurst Court a book was published called *The Feet of Young Men*, under the pseudonym of 'Janitor'. This was a study of the contemporary scene in the form of pen-sketches of prominent personalities, and a chapter entitled 'Two Brothers' was focused upon my uncles Alan Northumberland and Eustace Percy, with a lightly filled-in background of the whole of my mother's family. Dr Vaughan-Evans lent me this book, undoubtedly in a spirit of mischief combined with a hope that I might see my relations as others saw them, for 'Janitor's' criticism was tempered by no awe for the Percy Throne. The book fascinated me, for it was the first time I had heard unbiased adult appraisal of people who were part of my tiny circle of acquaintance. One of the opening paragraphs forced upon my attention the fact that the aunts and uncles whom we mimicked with such affectionate glee were genuinely not entirely like other people, a thought that had never occurred to me in that form.

'The Percies are a remarkable family, famous through many centuries of English history, and the present generation shows no sign of deterioration in the tradition. Its members are a Peculiar People, quite unlike anyone else, not exactly inhuman, but distinctly non-human.' I pondered this, and came to the conclusion that if it were true then I was distinctly non-human too, for with the exception of Uncle Alan Northumberland, whom we saw comparatively rarely, I felt myself both stimulated by them and in tune with them. In reading this chapter (skipping discussions of political issues that were far beyond my grasp) I was exercising conscious criticism of the written word for the first time in my life, and it was a curious and absorbing sensation.

The image of Aunt Muriel was brief but adequate. 'Lady Muriel, the youngest sister, is interested in protoplasms, especially in those which no one else has ever studied. She pays little attention to her clothes, and, like the Duke, is pale and red-haired. She is reported to have said once in sepulchral tones: "I can't think why people are given solitary confinement as a punishment. It is my idea of absolute bliss." ' I tried the sentence out in her deep drawl, and it was perfect, a worthy addition to the collection. And yet there was a false quantity; how could this ambition be reconciled with the enormous warmth that emanated from her mere presence in a room?

Aunt Victoria's paragraph also struck a false note somewhere. 'The story is told of Lady Victoria Percy, the present Duke's eldest sister and an expert on furs, that when studying her favourite subject she was much too busy to eat at regular times, but had a plate of ham always kept on the hall table so that she could snatch a morsel hastily in passing without interrupting her more pressing activities.'

It was quite impossible for me to reduce the image of my aunt to that of 'an expert on furs'; somehow it was derogatory. When we were not at Elrig, we shared with her a house in Albury village; she had converted the big sloping field between the house and the road into a gigantic Chinchilla rabbit farm, and no doubt she did know a lot about Chinchilla rabbit furs, but as an adjectival phrase qualifying her name 'an expert on furs' just wouldn't do. Packed with energy and initiative despite her *petite* and very demure exterior, she spent practically the whole day among the great encampment of creosote-wooden houses that held battalions, brigades and divisions of silvery rabbits; certainly her appearances at meals were irregular, and as she was happier with a plate of baked beans than with an elaborate dish they were usually limited to one course; but I didn't know anything about this plate of ham, and there would have been no point in leaving it in the hall, for the house was small and another four paces would have carried her into the dining-room.

The portrait presented of Uncle Eustace I found largely unrecognizable. 'The fairies who attended his christening – if we can imagine such creatures of fancy hovering over the cradle of an infant Percy – bestowed upon him many gifts; a fine intellect, high principle, ability, integrity, good temper and good looks; but, capriciously, they withheld from him the qualities – quite as valuable to a mortal – of humour, imagination and personal magnetism.' I was absolutely certain that whatever other qualities the fairies might have withheld they had not withheld humour, for one of our favourite imitations was of his great booming laugh that seemed so much too big for his body. Then 'Janitor' seemed to me to confuse him with Uncle Willie: 'He loves to argue for argument's sake, and whatever his real opinion may be, must always take the opposite view to the other person's. Time after time he will twist, shuffle, fence with words and shift his ground rather than admit agreement on the smallest detail.' I was quite unaware of this, having reserved the title of verbal chess champion for Uncle Willie ('perhaps the most human – by which I do not mean commonplace – of them all'), but I did just recognize: 'He will wear the same serious and intense air and use words of the same number of syllables whether he is addressing his two-year-old daughter or outlining educational policy to his colleagues and subordinates.' Only a year before, when I was not yet thirteen, he had described someone to me as 'one of the few coins that ring true in a singularly debased currency'.

But the ensuing direct, forceful criticism affected me in the same sort of way as if I had bumped into a thick sheet of plate-glass without knowing it was there; it had never remotely occurred to me that these Olympian adults were subject to the same sort of criticism that appeared in my school reports, and the reading of these passages resulted in my applying, from then on, my own form of criticism to every adult I met. Whereas before this time I had relied on a favourable or un-favourable aura surrounding a stranger, I now began con-sciously to analyse the probable reasons for the aura, and to formulate words to express the reaction to myself.

Of Uncle Eustace, 'Janitor' wrote: 'Lord Eustace has made more than one glaring mistake while he has been in office, and has drawn upon himself harsh criticism, not only from his political opponents, but also from many on his own side.' (He doesn't seem to be getting on as he should with either the masters or the other boys.) 'Very few people seem to have confidence in his wisdom or judgement. He has no instinct for affairs. He will do the right thing, but at the wrong time and in the wrong way.' (He must learn to behave like other boys.) '[His opponents] can neither understand nor forgive the frigid, intellectual combativeness of Lord Eustace, particularly as behind it they are unable to detect any depth of feeling or conviction.' (A most disappointing term. He must learn to mix better with other boys and not to be so argumentative with the staff. He won't get into the first eleven this year – or any other year if he goes on like this; he is deplorably lacking in team spirit. He could do much better if he tried – he is not lacking in ability.)

In contrast with my attitude to these passages concerning my relations whom I knew more or less well, the pages devoted to my Uncle Alan Northumberland inspired in me a profound and avid curiosity, for, though he was my only god-father, I hardly knew him at all. At Albury we would some-times meet him at church, in company with his exquisitely beautiful wife my Aunt Helen (daughter of the Duke of Richmond and Gordon) and walk part of the way home with him, but on these occasions he usually walked a few paces ahead of us children, deep in conversation with my mother or with Uncle Eustace or Aunt Victoria; and since my baby years I had never stayed at any of his houses. He was slight and wiry, red-haired and red-moustached, with a curious lift to the outermost corner of his lower eyelids, which contrived to give him both a far-sighted and slightly aggressive expression. In addressing us momentarily he seemed intensely good-willed but shy, in contrast to the perfect, Marie-Antoinette (whose pearls she owned) graciousness of Aunt Helen. Her extraordinary porcelain beauty of face and of figure, together with her apparent ineffectuality in any practical matter, made me (nourished on Stanley Weyman and Baroness Orczy) believe her destined for some plebeian guillotine as yet undevised; she must be slain alone, not in company with her peers, for in my mind she could have none.

'Janitor' appeared to feel an unwilling admiration for Uncle Alan, the kind of admiration that one might feel for an anachronistic Crusader who remained convinced of the desirability of conquering the Holy Land.

'He must be almost the first duke to practise journalism on an impressive scale. He writes articles for the *Patriot*, an obscure but bellicose periodical whose readers are deafened once a week by the buzzing of bees in the editorial bonnet. All who differ from him are "enemy agents in the pay of Russia". His letters are usually of the kind that the wise often write but only the unwise ever send off. They abound in the clichés of invective; so that after you have read one, each subsequent letter carries a familiar echo. "Such-and-such move on the part of the Labour party (or the Trades Unions or the Government or the Liberals or almost anybody) has inspired all decent law-abiding citizens with loathing and contempt." "The working man must be as sick of it as is every other right-thinking person (or right-minded body of men). . . ." "Common sense," he once remarked, "is the heritage of all men, however humble or unlearned." Though neither humble nor unlearned, he has yet to come into his heritage.'

But the next paragraph seemed to equate him, as in the case of Uncle Eustace, with the triumphant chess championship of Uncle Willie, giving substance to my wish for the whole Percy personality to pivot upon the character I knew and admired most. A clergyman 'had made a personal attack on him, declaring himself in favour of the confiscation of mining royalties without compensation, and an enemy of "the system of privileges and prerogatives by a class for a class who are descendants of Norman freebooters", etc. This is the kind of fly to which the Duke infallibly rises. Snatching up his pen, he rushed into battle with the rash cleric. Freebooters indeed! And if they were, had they not endowed the Church? And if they had, were not the clergy receivers of stolen goods, which they had no intention of giving up? "You denounce the present system; the Church is part and parcel of it, and you are making a very good thing out of it. You condemn feudalism; the Church is a relic of feudalism. You condemn privileges, and are yourself of a privileged caste. You condemn prerogatives, and the Church bristles with them." '

My heart under the badge of my school blazer swelled and reached out to him; attack was certainly the best form of defence.

'He is, as is well known, one of the largest [coal] royalty owners in England. Most people in such a position would feel themselves disqualified from taking an active part in a dispute on the rights and wrongs of coal royalties: they would prefer to leave their defence to others. Not so the Duke. He must be his own champion; he must defend not only the economics but even the ethics of his position; and no false delicacy will deter him from identifying his royalties with the common weal, or from calling his critics knaves or fools, or very possibly both. . . . Such was his tremendous sincerity that, in spite of ourselves, we were impressed – as though the tiger had himself appeared on the platform to plead against extinction. His Grace, perhaps, was not quite a tiger, but he had at least the appearance and the ferocity of a large and articulate ferret.'

This last sentence really shocked me, but it shocked me in such a way that I burst out laughing with the sheer outrage of it; it had never occurred to me to make such comparisons in the case of any adult, and that someone could write this of the head of the House of Percy seemed like a Hurst Court boy shouting out some schoolboy insult at Dr Vaughan-Evans in class. The curious thing was that I immediately identified myself with 'Janitor', and began at once to try to find animal counterparts for the masters. With some I was successful (Mr Curtis was a very fine and friendly gorilla) but I bogged down on Dr Vaughan-Evans. The nearest I could get was a black panther, but it wouldn't fit his unworthy body with its little round pot-belly.

When I gave the book back to him his mischief positively crackled from the harsh sallow face and great grey eyes. He said: 'Well – what did you think of it?'

'How much of it is true, sir?'

'That is a strange question. The answer is what I had hoped *you* were going to tell *me*. What did you come to Hurst Court for?' (He must have rehearsed this in advance.)

'To learn to think, sir,' I replied dutifully.

'Good. Well, you may keep the book if it helps towards that end. But perhaps it would be tactful not to tell your mother how you came by it.' And, to me incredibly, he winked.

Every Saturday Dr Vaughan-Evans gave us a spelling test. The words were carefully enunciated, the pupils spelled out on a sheet of foolscap their interpretation. At the end, the head-master read out the correct spelling, and each boy was trusted to call out the number of mistakes he had made. They were trusted to speak the truth, and I never knew of anyone cheating. I never made any mistakes, so when my name was called I replied 'Nought' in what had always been a treble or mezzo-soprano voice. One Saturday the word came out, by no intention, in the bass key. It was so bass as to cause me acute embarrassment as soon as that peculiar sound was loosed upon the air. Dr Vaughan-Evans raised his face from the desk, where he had been ticking off names, and said: 'Again?' I tried again, and it came out the same, like Paul Robeson in an idle moment. He looked at me with his standard technique of huge unblinking eyes and said: 'The pitcher seems to have gone to the well once too often.' Then his eyes flickered down and he went on with his list: 'Nugent? Prior? Rough? Soronoff? Wright? Young?'

When this happened I was thirteen and three months. Soon afterwards I was asked to attend the headmaster's study half an hour before our bedtime. Clouds of pipe-smoke and mental panic. Had I noticed any changes in my body recently? No, sir. Well, I hadn't: I had ignored them. Was I growing hair? Well, yes, I was. 'Well, that's a change, isn't it?'

This was my first sex talk. Whether it was because from the outset I connected it with what he had said about Craith, I closed my mind to it all, and assimilated hardly a word. I daresay he was explicit enough, but adults forget that, in the face of confusing situations, children have an almost miraculous power of making their minds go quite blank, and that was what I did. Towards the end of the talk I knew I was being warned against something, but I didn't know what. Occasionally he would ask: 'Did you know that already?' and always I answered yes, though I had not heard the previous sentence. I knew nothing, either before he started or after he had finished. The next day people asked me what V.-E. had wanted me for, and I said it was something about holiday arrangements with Mr Curtis. Other boys would emerge from these talks with their eyes dark with unwanted knowledge, or bright with suppressed excitement, or holding a mixture of fear and shame; I felt nothing but relief at an uncomfortable half-hour passed.

There were times after that when what Dr Vaughan-Evans had politely called the changes in my body became so noticeable and so embarrassing that I wished very much that I had listened carefully to all he had to say, but I realized that I could hardly ask him to repeat it all again, and as far as I ever knew sex was an absolutely taboo subject of conversation among the boys.

When I left Hurst Court the following summer, having passed my exams to go to Stowe in the autumn, my mother presented me with a book called *What a Young Boy Ought to Know*, but this did nothing to clarify matters; indeed it thickened the mystery into pea-soup. I came across the very book at Monreith recently, so I am able to quote from it verbatim – a cloud of verbal smoke as dense and obscuring as the pipe-puffing of Dr Vaughan-Evans. It had been published in 1912 by two doctors who had somehow escaped certification as insane, and as the book apparently sold like hot cakes they must have caused misery to an incalculable number of boys.

132

I open it at an early page and read: 'God in his infinite wisdom has ordained that...' Follows a modest account of how a male fish fertilizes eggs already laid by the female. 'These are examples of cases where the female eggs are fertilised and started into growth by the male cells *after* the eggs have been laid by the female. The way in which the female eggs are fertilised by the male before they are laid by the mother as in the case of birds, etc., we cannot now attempt to explain to you. What we have told you is very mysterious and very interesting. No-one can tell exactly what life is or how it is implanted in us.... Some unseen and unknown power causes the changes which occur and which end in the formation of a baby animal. You may read in the Bible that in the beginning God "created" man, male and female created He them. You must accept this as all that is known, and you must accept what we have told you about the way all life is handed on from parents to children as being all that you can know about it. But we want you to think about it as a marvellous and sacred thing. Before continuing, we are going to ask you to take for granted that what we have already told you is true, and we do not want you to start wondering about all these things....

'And you will remember that all these parts which we have described' (*the authors had forgotten at this point that they had not described any parts at all*), 'to you are called the private parts? You must regard them as private. No-one should see them but yourself' (*useful preparation for public school life, this*), 'and no-one but you should ever touch them. You must be modest in this respect, and you should know that if any other person touches you there that person is indecent and nasty-minded. No matter who it is, you should say to him: "That belongs to me; you have no right to touch it." ' (*I remembered, but fortunately did not act upon, these instructions during my medical examination on arrival at Stowe; it would have made a fine entry line.*) 'Self-abuse ... harm to the body and harm to the mind ... a boy will not feel so vigorous and springy; he will be more easily tired; he will not have so

133

good an eye for games ... will look pale and pasty ... indigestion ... spots and pimples ... follow a boy into his life and make him more likely to contract diseases. ... It is not too much for a doctor to say that a large number of boys and men are delicate for the reasons we have explained to you, and it is quite certain that a very large number of nervous people attribute their ailments to former self-abuse.' (*What do you expect, good doctor; if they had read your book how could they escape neurosis?*) But more, and worse: 'When it escapes from the body the body suffers, and so does the mind ... if from the habit of self-abuse the semen is never allowed to collect and produce its healthy effect, the brain and mind suffer severely. ... A boy like this is a poor thing to look at. ... He will probably be bottom of his class and get many a licking. He will surely be a duffer at games, and it is a hundred to one he gets laughed at more than any boy in the school for his blundering stupidity.' (*A masterpiece in confusion of cause and effect.*) 'Here again you must not forget that these disastrous conditions follow him into life, and as we have already impressed on you that what we have told you is *true*, you know now the harm that self-abuse does to the body and mind ... it is sure to injure him in his body, mind and character. He will discover this later on, when it is too late, and he will have to regret it all his life.' And beyond it, the witch-doctor implies, but his final assertion of power is still to come. He can read your thoughts. 'The eyes have been fancifully called "the windows of the soul". You see out of them, and others see into them. Keep these windows clean; when people see dirty windows they naturally conclude that the interior of the house is dirty, and its occupants too. Your mind and your soul are almost the same thing, and a dirty mind or soul does not bear thinking about. It is not a nice thing for anybody to see looking out of a boy's eyes. ... We want to remind you again that you have the promise of a doctor that he has told you the truth, and if boys laugh at you you have the satisfaction of knowing that *you* are right and *they* are wrong.'

And if you've taken all that in, my boy, you are now a fully blown member of the Flat Earth Society, and entitled to all its pleasures and privileges upon this flat earth and in the flat heaven beyond.

In my end-of-term French essay on what we hoped to do in the holidays I wrote that I hoped to *pécher* in error for *pêcher*, but the hope was not fulfilled; nor, on account of the good doctors' book, was it for a further two years.

9

THE GHOST OF MY FATHER

I HAVE LEFT it until now to introduce the ghost of my father, because it was not until this late stage that the dead overtly took over from the living. I interpret him now as being one of the great host covered by R. F. Mackenzie's phrase 'an untapped wealth of creative ability damped down and finally obliterated by the standard educational system'; and although the words are intended to describe another system, that of modern State education, they could only apply with still greater force to my father's upbringing. In everything that he left behind him I detect a struggle for conformity to the *mystique* of a small cult, without whose symbols and rituals he would have experienced a *horror vacui*. In order to conform, all possible originality of thought or action had rigorously to be suppressed, for to fellow-members of the cult all such things were suspect. Before going any further, it is perhaps time to define the cult. Basically, it was that of the sporting country squire, but to that comparatively simple concept was added extreme aristocracy, extreme self-sufficiency in practical matters, and an almost Prussian idolatry of His Majesty's Brigade of Guards. A Scottish member of this cult would not necessarily have been expected to hunt (though an earlier generation of Maxwells not only kept a pack of foxhounds at Monreith but also contrived to win the St Leger from their racing-stables there), but he would have been expected to be an outstandingly good shot, and to appear (on leave from one of the Household Brigade regiments) at most of the great shoots that flourished in Edwardian times, such as Holkham, Six Mile Bottom, Wemmergill and so on. At these houses he would meet replicas, externally at any rate, of himself (except for my Uncle Willie, who could never have been a replica of anybody), wearing the same kind of moustache and the same kind of Norfolk-jacketed knickerbocker suits cut in Savile Row. (Their personal possessions of leather were made of pigskin and lettered with name and regiment; everything of metal was silver – gold was vulgar – and carried a crest with initials below it. The same applies to my father's ivory shaving-brush.) Their guns were pairs – or trios – of Purdeys or Holland and Holland Royals, and they would all secretly vie to be included in a Society paper's list of the best twelve shots in the country. They would, naturally, keep records of the bags at these shoots in handsomely, even extravagantly, bound Game Books. In my father's massive white-and-gilt vellum edition, or in a later pigskin volume much heavier than the family Bible, he would enter the names of the party (say a week's grouse-driving at Totem Castle) after this manner:

Marquis of Boot	Scots Guards
Earl of Dubbin	Scots Guards
Lord Robert Kantish-Blimp	Grenadier Guards
Sir Rolf Pain-Gallstone	Coldstream Guards
The O'Callaghan of the Breeks	Irish Guards
Sir Digby Lightly-Fetheringham, Bt.	Welsh Guards
Hon. Hew Monday-Tuesday-Wednesday	Grenadier Guards
A.E.M.	Grenadier Guards

Under the heading 'Remarks' there may be some such throw-away line as 'Ld. Dubbin knocked out by a falling grouse', or 'The O'Callaghan retired with a headache after lunch'.

The military gods thus appeased, whatever artistic ability the member possessed could be devoted to embellishing the page (but *not*, mark you, to painting a drowning Ophelia in a bath or the martyrdom of St Sebastian – as in medieval times religion was the most acceptable art subject, and in modern totalitarian countries the State takes its place, so in this cult all talent had to be canalized into the cause). One could begin, say, by illuminating the Marquis of Boot's coat of arms in the top left-hand corner of the page, and by writing the words Totem Castle in an elaborate tricoloured Gothic script. These

137

possibilities exhausted, there is the whole 14 by 8 inch facing page of expensive cartridge-paper to decorate with drawings of grouse, caricatures of the party and whatever photographs are available. Thus the Game Book becomes a fetish in itself, the focal point of the cult, rather than a mere aid to memory, just as illuminated manuscripts became the magnet point of monastic culture. Everything that the Game Book contained became a symbol of security, a reassurance of membership, and it was therefore an entirely suitable repository for any unused talent in its owner's possession. The route by which one reaches this extraordinary position in the general maze I know, because I arrived at exactly the same point myself, and kept a huge and richly decorated fetish Game Book. It was not until after I was myself an officer in the Brigade of Guards, and well set for my father's mould, that I heard the remark: 'I see that at the end of the year 1907 your father recorded with apparent pride that he had been present at the killing of some 23,000 small birds and rodents.' (This was the figure following the decorated red-and-black words 'Grand Total'.) 'Was this total really so very grand?'

He possessed a number of books, but despite an armorial bookplate among whose copious mantling twined a scroll bearing the words: 'These are my friends; age cannot wither them nor custom stale their infinite variety', the subject-matter was in fact largely confined to sport and military history. I believe my father, like myself, to have been initially endowed with at least average talent and sensitivity – possibly more than average sensitivity, or he would not have bothered to have plated himself with so thick and ostentatious an armour of Guards, guns and group symbols. A partial awareness of this situation is evidenced by a quotation inscribed on the fly-leaf of his largest and most magnificent Game Book: 'In those uncivilized days, the arts of war and hunting constituted the only employment of the great; their active but uncultivated minds were susceptible of no pleasures but such as were of a violent kind, procured exercise for their bodies, and charmed away the languor of reflection.' (Osbaldeston on the Saxon

Kings.) There are other signs of something trying to burst out of its tightly buttoned scarlet uniform, only to be prodded back by the officer commanding the super ego. In a profusion of heavy, half-bound manuscript books he was always writing things down, or rather beginning to. One of these is titled on the fly-leaf, in his rounded but curiously stylized handwriting, *A Book of Dreams*. On the following page is an introductory note, in the mandarin style of my grandfather, explaining that as dreams are so quickly forgotten they should be recorded immediately, and this he has now resolved to do. Remembering that this volume antedates Freud's earliest publication by some years, the reader turns eagerly forward in search of revelation – only to find that the whole manuscript book is blank beyond the first page. Another, obviously inspired by my grandfather's most popular work *Memories of the Months*, is already divided into twelve sections labelled January to December, but contains only a brief handful of notes concerning wildfowl on the shore. A number of the manuscript books have been begun as diaries, but they rarely contain any consecutive entries, and most of these have been written in anger. A leaf of one of these books is headed *Mine intimate acquaintance*. There follows a list of five names, whose owners had the same seemingly strictly limited sphere of interests as he himself, but a firm red line has been drawn through two of them. Now, it seems to me that an essential difference between my father and the possibly crashing bores enumerated in his list is that they would not have felt the necessity to make a written inventory of their friends, much less under so curiously arch a heading, and certainly they would not have kept the inventory abreast of current breakages.

What was my father? From my mother I knew only that he was a brilliant shot, a brave soldier, and that he had faultless manners towards women; the last of these attributes, proffered as an object of emulation, became unconsciously fused with the first two, so that all three appeared as necessary qualifications for adult life. A child does not question these things; I did not, during my boyhood, try to give any precise shape to the figure that had worn all those gaudy uniforms that were behind glass in the schoolroom wall, whose face above the epitaph of official dispatch looked down from above the chimney-piece, who had played the presentation set of bagpipes which were in a glass case in the hall, and whose ghost was strong in every room in the house.

As a child in school groups he looks listless and unhappy, and from fragments of writing it seems that he experienced then and for long after the same nostalgic hankering for Monreith as I did for Elrig. He was taken away from Eton when he was sixteen and sent to the crammer at Newport Pagnell with whom thirty years later I spent dreary Sundays from Stowe – to learn what he had failed to learn at Eton; what my grandfather, also removed at sixteen, had failed to learn at Eton; what I, removed from Stowe at sixteen, had failed to learn there. Evidently we were all unsuitable school material. From Mr Trevor's cramming establishment he passed into Sandhurst and from Sandhurst into the Grenadier Guards. The flavour of his existence is imparted by scraps of essay and diary, through which run the old nostalgic theme, the ecstasy of greeting, at Monreith, his current Labrador retriever, Raven, at the end of an eighteen-hour journey from Aldershot or Pirbright. Like my mother, he hankered to escape from his rituals and uniforms; unlike her, and I suspect partly because his religious beliefs were less massively founded than hers, he found himself adrift without them, and was always, without confidence, awaiting the beginning of something absolutely new, some precious metal recognizable without a hallmark.

He fought in the Boer War, got a bullet through his clothing that left him unwounded, and returned to England to retire from the Army. Then, with four of his brother-officers familiar from the Game Book (Hon. R. Coke, Hon. E. Coke, Hon. Gerald Legge and H. Russell Stephenson) he went to Java and planted rubber. This, long after his death, proved a highly successful enterprise, whose fruits paid for a large portion of our education. He returned with recurrent malaria, took up again to the full his old hobby of shooting, and acquired from my grandfather the sporting rights over part of Monreith Estate. These he proceeded to develop with a single-minded efficiency, for to have followed him thus far is to realize that he was wholly and irrevocably dedicated to shooting. He was, as clearly, totally unqualified to earn a living except by the exploitation in some way of his hobby – if so devouring a passion can be described by that trivial word. He wrote three books *Grouse and Grouse Moors, Partridges and Partridge Manors* and *Pheasant in Covert and Aviary*, and contributed articles to sporting periodicals. The descriptive passages are vocative but not evocative ('you half turn as the rest of the covey goes whizzing by'); in fact you are not only told what to do but what you feel and what you have done and have felt, and what you will do and will feel. Unless one is a sporting painter, and one who enjoys a vogue among the priesthood of the cult, there is little further one can do to extract a livelihood from firing off twenty thousand cartridges a year at our feathered friends, as the friends, more particularly when reared especially for the purpose, do not even pay for their own destruction. There was, however, one more possibility; after he married my mother, my father started at Elrig a training-kennels for gundogs. (I considered doing the same, and at the age of eighteen served a brief apprenticeship with a famous gundog trainer.) It was not a happy venture, to judge by the records that remain, resulting in the full measure of acrimonious correspondence that is endemic to such establishments, and ending in an epidemic of distemper that killed his own dogs beside those of his clients.

All this time, it must be remembered, and ever since the death of his elder brother William in 1897, he had been heir to Monreith Estate, and with my mother's sizeable dowry there cannot have seemed any very pressing necessity to do anything but mark time. It would no doubt have seemed very improbable to him that twenty-five years later my brother would also be marking time, waiting to inherit from the same man.

I find it impossible to guess what would have happened had

141

there been no war and had he lived. He would have waited until 1937 before inheriting Monreith; our Church had the strongest prohibitions against contraception and my mother had produced four children in four years of marriage. There would assuredly have been an ugly population explosion, and I expect the half-dozen youngest sons would have been sent into the Army or into Colonial administration.

But the war came; my father joined the Royal Naval Division, and with his battalion of half-trained and faultily equipped recruits he was whisked overseas after a fraction of the time he had insisted to be necessary. He survived his landing in France by no more than two or three hours, being killed by the very first shell of the bombardment.

My grandfather wrote in his *Evening Memories*: 'Aymer has gone hence, whereby, among deeper reasons for regret, the links of family lore have been severed, which hitherto in this house had served to carry custom and tradition from father to son as the centuries rolled by.'

For reasons obvious enough in the circumstances my mother encouraged in her sons their father's interests, and this, to-gether with the aggregate of many, many hours alone in the company of Hannam the gamekeeper, had by the age of puberty produced in me a fervour for shooting that not even my father could have surpassed. I aspired to the cult if for no other reason than that it was the only cult of whose existence I was aware, and by the rifling of my father's tomb I had acquired the priestly, esoteric language and all the passwords. I saw no paradox in my genuine love of the creatures that I killed, nor did the division between 'game' and other birds appear to me arbitrary or reasonless. I questioned these things no more than I questioned the desirability of reading every night a set and incomprehensible portion of the Bible from our Church's Almanack.

10

A PALACE FOR THEIR PLEASURE

THE SUMMER holidays after I left Hurst Court, Elrig was let as usual, and we went abroad for the first time, to Brittany. Mr Curtis, whose father was the British Consul in Dinard, drove us from Saint-Malo in his ramshackle little Citroën. He would stick his great pear-shaped head out of the driver's window and boom at French pedestrians: 'Pour aller à Vannes?' 'Ah, merci *très* bien!' and eventually we arrived at a modest seaside hotel whose brochure described it as 'situated in an umbrageous park', which turned out to be a sparse and scruffy little grove of Mediterranean pines. Aunt Muriel came with us too. When in search of information she would approach a native with an apologetic and quizzical half smile and drawl: 'Pardon, Madame, mais nous sommes des Anglais.' 'Ça se voit!' was the merry retort that gave Aymer and me the giggles for several hours. We sailed in fishing-boats in the Morbihan Bay (deep blue, opaque waves and small pine-covered islands), caught lizards with Aunt Muriel, visited the standing stones of Carnac, and I made endless pencil-sketches of pastoral landscapes with church spires. Eustace brought his insect-collecting paraphernalia; and catching sight of a rarity alighted on a smart Frenchwoman's back he plucked it expertly into the killing bottle with a courtly: 'Pardon, Madame, mais vous avez une insecte sur les dos.' The only thing I remember about the hotel itself was the appalling smell of the lavatories (always occupied when one required them) which I put down to the French excretory system rather than to the plumbing.

At the end of the summer holidays I went to Stowe School. It was Britain's newest public school, having been open for less than five years, and as yet the minimum amount of alteration had been carried out to convert into a school the gigantic country mansion of the extinct Dukes of Buckingham and Chandos, as splendid and breath-taking a palace as ever a sovereign graced. The enormous and exquisitely beautiful park, little tended since the Comte de Paris's tenancy before the First World War (it reminded him of Versailles) was an unordered wilderness in which one came almost unaware upon Palladian follies, glorious temples and statues, isolated Grecian façades and noble arches; footpaths meandered by mighty cedars or through woodlands and thickets where now, disastrously, they run straight and tarmacadamed to modern and almost suburban staff quarters; the whole place, conceived

Stowe South Front

on a scale to rival Blenheim Palace, had a wildness, an abandon of beauty, that to me it could not have contained without this element of disarray.

The school, with its mere three hundred boys, had not had time enough to acquire the complex and meaningless set of rituals and intolerances that characterize the maturer institutions, and in those early days there were the minimum number of rules consistent with discipline. There were no 'bounds', all boys were allowed to keep dogs or any other pets they liked (I suppose the line would have been drawn short of elephants or lions, but no one put this to the test); to sail boats on the great ornamental lakes or to go for long walks or bicycle expeditions; and in the early days the attitude was permissive in general.

144

There was, however, an underlying note of hearty brashness that affected me the more for its juxtaposition with the classic grace of the great house and its exquisite parklands. This disharmony, akin I think to the unease one may sense when the public of other countries visit the state rooms of their dethroned monarchs, leading to an exchange of over-loud inanities, found its outward expression at Stowe in a positive babble of weak punning, a not infrequent symptom of incipient schizophrenia. Hence the school motto was 'Sto, persto, praesto' (I stand, I endure, I excel), and at roll-calls (called 'stances') in the great central circular marble hall, when the captain of each house would reel off the names of his seventy boys with the staccato speed of a motor-mower (Adam-sonAlingtonAshtonBrabyBrodieCallendar) we could answer not 'here' or 'present' but (I find myself blushing to write it) 'Sto'. Worse still, as members of the school we were Stoics, and those who had left were Old Stoics.

The school motto was also the refrain of the school song, which contained some acutely embarrassing lines. Opening with the comparatively innocuous stanza:

> *Temples and Grenvilles, Lords of Stowe,*
> *In spacious days of leisure*
> *Built far and wide on this hill-side*
> *A palace for their pleasure*

– and capering on with an increasingly beery lack of inhibition, it suddenly tripped and fell face downward into a pile of dirty cricket-flannels and test-match scores:

> *The world shall know the greater Stowe*
> *In this her second innings.*

The curriculum did not quite correspond with its manifesto. This stated that there were no compulsory games, which was simply not true. There were, perhaps, fewer than at most established public schools, but any compulsory game would have been preferable to the afternoons when the Captain of the House pinned on the notice-board the brief announcement:

'Run for all', and some sixty shivering boys wearing brief cotton shorts and singlets set off in an icy downpour for some distant destination such as the Obelisk. A mile each way was torture for a body geared to sprint.

The manifesto also claimed proudly that at Stowe there was no fagging. This was pure sophistry; it was called 'officing', and the only practical difference was that study-holders did not have a personal fag; all senior boys employed all junior boys to do their washing-up and charring. (Smell of sour dishcloths and the gritty rasp of Vim; in the wastepaper-baskets envelopes full of cigarette-ends and others sealed that we were forbidden to open – we obeyed and wondered, but I can now guess their contents.) But unlike most schools the senior boys were almost universally friendly to junior boys (not always, of course, without ulterior motive) and whatever bullying took place was almost invariably between contemporaries.

The whole driving force of Stowe was one man, just as at St Wulfric's it had been one woman. J. F. Roxburgh, always abbreviated in conversation to J.F., was the first headmaster of Stowe, and in any history of the British upper-class educational system he should loom large, greater than Arnold, because he was a man of eccentric brilliance who defied all conventions.

He was in his early thirties then (a bachelor, as he remained), by far the youngest headmaster of a public school ever to have been appointed, and because of his unusual qualities he had been chosen from Lancing to become the benign dictator of a new ideal. Apart from his attributes of scholarship and energy, he was a visually impressive figure by any standards. He stood about six foot two, had an odd head and affected odd clothes. He had wavy brown hair which he parted in the middle and oiled heavily, grey eyes, a large wavy nose and a humorous mouth. This head surmounted a highly individual sartorial effect: very well cut double-breasted tweed trouser suits (at least twenty of them) for the most part greyish or greenish with multiple semi-concealed overchecks; bright silk bow-ties; knife-edged trousers; blunt black ankle-boots of a polish so high that they looked like patent leather, and a rich Paisley pattern silk handkerchief usually jutting from his breast pocket. His manner was expansive, even in moments of crisis, his walk dynamic, and his speech forceful and multi-synonymous like the Psalms ('I find this room cold, chilly, frigid or of a temperature below that which is desirable. In other words it is not within the comfort zone on the Fahrenheit scale. *Moribund* Maxwell, would you be so good as to rise, stand, or otherwise become vertical and adjust that window, orifice or aperture so that it is closed, shut and hermetic?'). He possessed a memory for faces, names and related facts that would have earned him a handsome living as an entertainer; at that time, and I believe much later when the school had more than doubled its size, he knew by sight, full names and background, every boy in the school. On the last night of every term he would carry an electric torch round every dormitory after lights out and, using each boy's Christian name, wish him a happy holiday, usually making some reference to the boy's home or background. As our blatantly labelled trunks stood, on that last night, at the foot of each bed, we thought we had discovered the secret of how he cheated, and we changed all the trunks round so that the names upon them did not correspond with the name of the boy in the bed, but he ignored this ruse entirely and addressed us as before. Then we thought he had a memorized ground-plan of the beds themselves and we all changed beds on the last night, but that, too, had no effect; he seemed to rely entirely upon the pencil-beam of the torch upon a boy's face, to recognize it and to know all about its owner's history and family.

Despite his awe-inspiring array of positive qualities, J.F. either lacked absolutely the ability to select subordinates, or possibly because of a certain element of megalomania he would not tolerate a strong character on his staff. Almost without exception they were bachelors, and almost without exception they were either sycophants or comparative nonentities. During the time that I was at Stowe there were three masters who made a profound impression upon me, who made me feel the closeness of an adult human being, and of those three, two subsequently committed suicide. The rest were faintly alarming by their nominal authority; they ought to have commanded sympathy by their pathos, but in most cases they commanded only concerted mockery to the limit of our daring. Some of them were almost incredible. They were all young men. One who taught history walked with the feverish energy of some strange robot, his shoulders high and hunched, his limbs completely stiff, legs flung with each stride to the absolute limit of their travel, and the arm that was not encumbered with books rowing him frantically through the air on the pivot of his shoulder. Another, whose jowl needed shaving three times a day, tried some widely-advertised depilatory (or so it was rumoured) and turned a dark moss-green from cheekbone to collar line. I see the ill-adjusted features of a third (small, evasive brown eyes and curly brown hair far receded at twenty-six years) waving and weaving on his long neck as a cobra's head sways to the movements of its charmer. I see a chemistry master, dirty, bespectacled, dishevelled and balding, brewing up some hideous mixture in a retort; it seethes, rises and suddenly spews itself over the bench. From high on the tiered benches facing him a breaking voice yells: 'God, he's come!' The master wipes up the mess without comment.

Later, only just overlapping my time at Stowe, came the exotic eccentrics, the Birds of Paradise, with their scarlet cloaks and their supercharged Bentleys and their Baronies of the Holy Roman Empire; the most my own era could achieve in improbable combination was a music master who was also the local Master of Foxhounds.

A number escaped enmity because of their evident goodwill. My housemaster, for example, was an amiable and civilized retired clergyman, a bachelor, who had been headmaster of a preparatory school before he was persuaded by J.F. to abandon it and come to Stowe. He lasted only three years after my arrival; he disliked both responsibility and imposing discipline; and when he left the 'moral tone' of the house had

148

become so lax, not to say frankly luxurious, that a disciplinarian (addicted to riding and marriage) was put in to clean up,
and a number of boys were expelled. Some of those who were
not wrote a clerihew about this successor, which ended:

> *And now the House is so clean*
> *There's nothing to be seen*
> *But me and my horse*
> *And Mrs Cross.*

His amiable predecessor had enjoyed a friendlier verse:

> *Here only one man sleeps alone*
> And *never interferes;*
> *The parson never casts a stone*
> *And has not eyes nor ears.*

To this essentially sympathetic parson, with nervous brown
eyes and floppy grey hair, I was summoned during my first
few days at Stowe for a personal talk. It began with religion
and ended with sex, and my flimsy façade was disastrously
intact at the end of both. He had a white pocket-handkerchief
which he flipped aimlessly and energetically as he talked, as
though he were swatting invisible embarrassments that buzzed
round him like flies. Did I believe in a personal devil? (He
pronounced it 'dev-vil'.) I replied cautiously that if one believed in a personal God I didn't see why one shouldn't believe
in a personal devil. 'I'm very glad you have such definite views
about it, very glad indeed. Few boys have, in my experience.'
(Flick, flick.) 'Now, about sex.' (Flick.) 'Did the headmaster
of your preparatory school talk to you about it?' I said he had,
but didn't add that I hadn't listened. He was obviously relieved. 'Then I needn't say much about it.' He didn't, and
what he did say was quite a different line of approach. 'Take
great care of' (flick, flick, flick) 'that-part-of-the-body-
commonly-known-as-the-balls. Easily damaged, and you've
only got two. Always wear a box when playing cricket. If
you're fighting, see you don't get hit there. Keep yourself
clean.' He ended with some eminently sensible and hygienic

advice about local depilation (here the handkerchief knocked down a silver-framed photograph and a tobacco jar from the chimney-piece) which to me was unnecessary until a much later date. I was strangely unembarrassed, and I understood everything he said, but I was still both innocent and ignorant.

I was still frightened of numbers, and the numbers were very much greater than I had ever known before, but the landscape was so vast and the amount of free time so comparatively great that I was able, almost whenever I wanted, to revert to my old pastime of being alone. I was not only alone during my free afternoons, wandering farther and farther into this deep un-familiar English countryside of oaks and open pasture, copses and hazel spinneys, but I was also alone for the whole of the free time after breakfast every morning, for I was far too shy to use the House lavatories. These, known in the Stowe vocabulary as 'Egypt', were in a long row, quarter-doored and quarter-partitioned, so that they afforded a strictly token priv-acy, and this in my mind left me no choice but the woods, the infinite thickets of laurel and rhododendrons that stretched away in disorder from my detached House.

Later, before my public school career was abruptly cut short by illness at the age of sixteen, I found other boys as shy and rustic as I, boys who shared the interests in which I had been brought up, but inevitably during the first two terms I was thrown much in the company of the half-dozen new boys of my House. With them there were at first few points of contact, and I preferred to go for long walks in the cold autumn park-lands and by the withered sedges of the many lakes and streams, a landscape largely depopulated of wild life between September and April, but with enough migrant birds to bring it alive to me. Above all it was a wilderness; in such, though of a wilder kind, I had grown up, and in it I found enough sub-human creatures to form my chorus. (Even that first term, when an early snowfall came and ice coated the bare twigs of the trees, I cherished a tea-chest full of exhausted and starving Redwings – thrush-sized migrant birds which hopped help-

lessly in the snow, their breast-bones sharp and bare as knives
– and I spent my pocket-money on buying for them ants' eggs
and mealworms.)

The Reverend Earnest Earle made, as I have implied, little
impression upon me beyond a vague and gentlemanly benign-
ity; not so his second-in-command, who from my arrival at
Stowe made me aware of the full conscious impact of an adult
personality upon that of an adolescent. My under-housemaster
– whose face, voice and gestures I came to know so well during
the long hours in which he tried to break down a barrier
possessing the impregnability of utter innocence – was a man
in his mid-twenties, tall, slim, lithe, blue-eyed, possessing
what would have been almost excessive good looks had they
not been marred by near-albinism of the hair and eyebrows.
He had a charming smile, a gay laugh, and an easy confidential
manner; the charm that he could switch on like an electric
current was directed at me for nearly two years, but I did not
know what he wanted of me. Other people did; when he used
to send for me after bedtime to give me private coaching in,
say, Spanish, I thought they sniggered at my implied linguistic
backwardness rather than my inferred sexual forwardness.
Returning to bed through the darkened dormitory from which
his room led people would whisper to me: 'How did it go,
Maxwell?' But the innuendo was utterly lost upon me. He did
not know this; years later, and shortly before his early death,
he told a mutual acquaintance that he had thought my innocence assumed, and that my evident liking for his company
had prolonged inordinately an emotion of which he did not
want to be reminded. But in those early days, though I was
puzzled, I was flattered by his attentions; I did not distinguish
between shades of friendship, whether in boys or masters, nor
wonder overmuch why they were proffered. And my under-
housemaster, unique among his colleagues, was comfortingly
uncritical of my work.

I had been placed in a high form on my arrival at Stowe, with

151

nearly all the junior school below me. Unfortunately they would not stay there, and from leading by many lengths I was soon indisputably last of the field. I slid, like a towel slipping sluggishly from a towel-horse, to the bottom of the form of twenty-eight boys, and there or thereabouts I remained during my two years at Stowe. Two English masters and a teacher of biology struck ephemeral sparks from my dour flint, but the rest did not even attempt to relate to their pupils the apparently esoteric subjects they taught; I could not see what all these things had to do with me, and I closed my mind to them as effectively and completely as I had closed my mind to Dr Vaughan-Evans's no doubt illuminating sex talk. With few exceptions the masters' subject reports were of such uniform phraseology as to suggest collusion. 'He appears utterly incapable of any form of concentration.' 'He is not lacking in ability and could do better if he tried. Most disappointing.' They all got the pronoun wrong – it seemed to me that I could have done better if *they* had tried; they were paid to teach, and were presumed to have some aptitude for it, while I was not paid to learn. Reading those reports now I am reminded of words that I have quoted elsewhere in this book: 'I am convinced that there is an untapped wealth of creative and also of technical ability that is damped down and finally obliterated by the standard educational system.'

Where my mind was during those withdrawn form-room hours I remember quite well; most of the time I was at Elrig. I would begin with a brief ritual of self-hypnotism to erase the tiresome sound of voices and meaningless words. Ever since I was a small child I had visualized the calendar as a clock-face, with Christmas at about twelve o'clock and my birthday, July 15th, a few minutes after half past six. Each month was a segment of the circle, as spectrum colours are represented on a disc, and each month had its own colour, a colour dictated by the vowels the name of the month contained. Consonants had no colours, or rather they were uniformly dark, but the vowels had hues pervasive enough to stain a whole world with their dye: a, green; u, mauve; o, white; e, ochre; i, black; y,

152

yellow. I would select a month at random (I cheated because I wanted to be at Elrig in the spring or summer) and I would then set off from the house for a walk calculated to last the whole of the forty-five-minute form period.

From the inside I turned the heavy twisted ring of iron that opened the side-door by the gun-room and stepped down one of the big raw flagstone steps before I turned to close it behind me (rust on the outside iron ring, and a smell of creosote from the heavy, nail-studded wood of the door). Outside it is sunny, and there are big cumulus clouds lazing high across a pale blue sky. I turn to the right, sandals crunching on fine granite chips, and tiptoe lest my form master hear me and call me back. Then I am past the east wing of the house and on to a grass-grown track, the slow thudding of the diesel generator in the garage becoming fainter behind me. After a hundred yards I reach the dry stone wall that is the boundary of our enclave. There is a farm gate here of weathered wood, but the hinges have gone, and to save the bother of lifting the gate I vault it. In front of me the track fords a little stream before reaching, thirty yards on, another ramshackle gate in another dry stone wall. (When we were small we used to call this enclosure 'between-the-two-gates', and we caught minnows and stickle-backs in the stream.) Beyond the second gate the track forks, to the left high over the moor before descending to the heathery wastes of the Mochrum Lochs, and to the right it can lead into Aireylick farmyard or, bearing left again, it runs along the side of a ragged, wind-blown fir wood – the Fey Wood, or Fairy Wood; with the heather moor of our nursery picnics at the left, and at the right a tumbling moss-grown wall that defines the edge of the wood. There is bracken at both sides of the track, and the flash of rabbit scuts. From the wood comes the dreamy cooing of woodpigeons, and some-times the brief cardboard clatter of their wings.

Forty-five minutes, and five gone already. I'll play fair, as I used to when as a nine-year-old I set off alone along that track with a hunter chiming watch in my sporran; I'll be back for lunch. Sometimes I go through the wood, clambering painfully

153

over a fifty-foot fallen larch overgrown with brambles (tall foxgloves, dark-spotted in their intimate interiors, pink velvet in my lady's chamber). Nests, hawks, owls, the lone bare-trunked Scots pine in whose needled summit rested, poised, our rarity (so common elsewhere) – a carrion crow's nest. No, not today, not during maths – the climb will take too long. Leave the wood, over the moss-grown stones of its wall, and resume the grass-grown track. At the end of the wood the track ends, abruptly, with another farm gate. Leaning on it I look out over a long, declining grassy field, isolated between rough hills and heather, a foreground deeply peopled with childhood. Beyond its few acres stretch at first the untameable peat-bogs of Galloway (flat, alternating dark brown of cut peat and lighter mauve-brown of heather – ten miles or more of these), then low arable fields and beyond them again, twenty miles away, the huge pale blue whale-back shapes of the Galloway Hills, Cairnsmore of Fleet, Cairnsmore of Carsphairn, Ben Iolaire and the dimly towering peak of The Merrick. The foreground field was part of our small years, we called it 'the mushroom field', because in it grew a profusion of huge horse-mushrooms (many of them spored and black below, tunnelled by small soft white maggots; 'after all, they're only made of mushroom, it doesn't make any difference'). On the left upward slope of this field, close to a great pile of stones eliminated from the arable by generations of Wigtown plough-men, stands a wind-distorted hawthorn some twenty feet high, and in the varying density of its topmost branches is dis-cernible the hooded basket of a magpie's nest. I cover the quarter-mile between gate and tree in a matter of seconds, and at once I am climbing. Thorned branches stick in my clothing, spines draw blood on hands and knees. The final approach to any birds' nest was an affair of struggle and achievement. My hand reaches through the twigged zareba of basket and basket handle, touches the soft lining, touches the firm intimacy of the eggs . . .

'MAXWELL!'

The scene dissolves, slowly, and I am looking at an almost apoplectically angry Stowe master in a Stowe form-room. The one who comes to my mind is Mr Brace, a handsome black-haired young dandy who tried (or did he?) to teach me mathematics. Perhaps he did; I still can't do long division, but it has not been a crippling handicap in life. His hair is black, his face is red with anger above bizarrely long silk collar-points which I tried to copy when I reached Oxford a few years later.

'Sir?'

'What have I just said, Maxwell?'

'I don't know, sir.' (I was always honest on this point, but it only made things worse.)

More than once his rage was so great as to request me to leave the room at once, but I was 'protected' by my under-housemaster and no disaster ensued. I didn't want to challenge him; in fact I admired him, which was not true of my Latin master, a little pince-nezed Himmler of a man with mincing voice and industrial-urban clothes.

. . . left this time, from the gun-room door, across the gritty drive (one of my sister's goats is at tether on the far side, and bleats to be allowed to follow), through the tunnelled hawthorn shrubbery we knew as Mother's Den, through the water garden and over the stone wall that divides it from the steep open moor beyond. For the first hundred yards or so the slope is thick with the crisp, rust-red bracken of last year; it is like walking through cornflakes. The pale green rods and curled, heraldic heads of the new growth are pushing up through the foot-deep layer of the old. The world is full of birds' voices; below me as I climb, the rooks come and go from the elm clump, above me on the hill a curlew trills a steadily ascending scale '*Wharp – wharp – wharp wha-a-up – wha---a-up*', a lark is singing at some invisible point overhead. Up from the bracken on to the short, bare heather, springy heather under my young, springy feet, up on to the ridge that rises at its northern end to the High Cairn. At the summit of the ridge a grouse whirrs up out of the heather with a cackle, steadies its wings stiffly and slides smoothly round the shoulder of the hill. The sea is in sight now, a glittering high horizon; the sense of space is enormous, and holds in it something near to rapture. The warm wind that ruffles the heather tops has the salt tang on it mingled with the moorland smells. Between the moor and the sea stretches a long, shallow valley; at its sides are steep fields of poor arable dotted with hawthorn trees, but the valley is neither arable nor heather. It is choked with thorn trees, many of them densely overgrown with ivy, so that the stream that runs through them, clear amber water over small pebbles, is as guarded as any sacred spring. The valley is called Changue Glen, and I was told that my father called it the Happy Valley. To me, too, it is an enchanted place; I set out down the longer heather slope to enter its mysteries, perhaps even to reach the sea.

I am recalled by a sharp pain at the back of my neck. Turning sharply I find my Latin form master standing over me, tweaking the hair at my nape. 'Maxwell, you will remain after the bell has gone and discuss education with me.' I did, and given this opportunity, he twisted my ear, pulled the short hair at the back of my neck, and made some very insulting remarks. At the end of these he said thinly: 'Well, what have you got to say?' For some reason I didn't properly understand I replied through hardly-repressed tears: 'Maxima debetur puero reverentia.' He dropped my ear as though he had received an electric shock, and walked away the length of the form-room. Then he turned, adjusted his pince-nez, and asked: 'Who taught you that phrase?' There was no curiosity in his voice.

'You, sir, last week.'

And in his sallow, thin-lipped voice he replied: 'And of all the classic dicta I have tried to teach, that is all you remember? I should have expected as much.'

Later, he discovered brandy.

I spent the evening hours of preparation in very little greater application to the set subjects than I passed the form-room

156

hours, but with a variation. Preparation took place in the 'house-room', the room communal to all boys not yet old enough to have a study, and was invigilated by a master or prefect every evening from 7.45 until 9.45. I discovered

From a drawing by a Stowe
Contemporary of the author with a little Owl.

almost immediately that under the eyes of an invigilator who had not even the distraction of teaching it was difficult or impossible to get away with pure day-dreaming; one had to appear absorbed in some book that was a school-book. There was only one of the slightest interest to me, and that was the collection of verse entitled *The Golden Treasury*. I learned a fresh poem from it every day or two, writing them out after I had closed the book, so as to provide a full show of industry, and when I left Stowe I think I knew the whole *Golden Treasury* by heart, though I had learnt little else.

11

SO MANY MISUNDERSTANDINGS

STOWE WAS my first realization of the depth, the languorous luxuriance, the immensity of green foliage and yardlong hay, that makes an English summer in the shires. That summer when I became fifteen was the very first time I had ever seen it; true I had spent four summers at school in England, but nothing in the suburban atmosphere of Heddon Court nor in the barely covered chalk of the Sussex Downs had prepared me for this incredible, voluptuous lushness, as remote from the windswept moorlands of Elrig as a tropical rain forest. I was fascinated by it, half repelled and half drawn, certainly not indifferent; it remains connected in my mind with vague stirrings and unknown longings, as if I equated this sappy landscape with the body of a lover.

In view of my extremely emotional nature it was surprising that I spent two whole years at Stowe without once falling in love. I was aware that most of the boys did, even dimly conscious that some were from time to time in love with me, but as the whole concept was still foreign to me I had no criteria for diagnosing the condition in others. I was intensely aware of beauty, and a face that I found beautiful would hold my attention completely for as long as it was in view, but I was unaware of any feeling of active attraction, and I never made any attempt to know the owners of the faces.

The only real friendship that I formed outside my own House foundered on the, to me, uncharted rocks that had threatened my partnership with Craith at Hurst Court, and for as little reason. I can't remember how I first met Fernhurst; he was a pleasant-looking boy, fair-haired and freckled, more than two years older than I was. He belonged to one of the

Houses in the main building, and he shared the majority of my interests and enthusiasms. Since we did not naturally meet without rendezvous, we were always waiting for each other at some pre-arranged meeting-place, outside the Chapel, or at the bicycle-sheds, or by this or that pergola or temple in the woods. To me it seemed an easy, undemanding friendship, and we went for long birds-nesting walks and bicycle rides during the whole of the first summer term, but the eye of prejudice had us squarely in its sights, waiting for excuse to pull the trigger. Prejudice in this case was represented by a peculiarly loathsome young thug of eighteen – Ruprecht is as good a name as any other – who later became one of Mosley's body-guard, a job for which, being all brawn and aggression, he was eminently suited. He had, we found out later, been following us for a week or more, spying from behind trees and ruins, determined to discover what it was that Fernhurst saw in my company.

On the occasion when he found enough excuse to pounce, we were looking for Little Owls' nests in the park adjoining the Stowe boundaries, the property of a Mr Robart, squire of a lesser but substantial house and domain. It was a huge park, grazed by a dwindling herd of fallow deer, and dotted with archaic clumps of oaks and chestnut trees. We had, as boys do, become languid under the afternoon sun, and lying in the shade of a lightning-riven oak Fernhurst had introduced me to cigarettes. My first was a failure; it reminded me of the smoke in Mr Stallard's study and being beaten with a cricket-bat, and I stubbed it out after a few puffs. Fernhurst mocked me, delicately gentle, and went on smoking his. Ruprecht somehow contrived to spring down from the tree itself, landing directly before us with his hands on his hips and his odious cropped skull and pale eyes smashing us as later his brass knuckle-dusters smashed the jaws of aged and fragile dissenters.

'Ha! Caught you! Smoking on Mr Robart's land!'

Something of the oddness of the sentence struck me even at the moment; I couldn't see what Mr Robart's land had to do with it. Smoking was against the school rules; Mr Robart didn't enter into them. Both Fernhurst and I were too taken aback to do or say anything.

'Your names? You!' Ruprecht addressed Fernhurst.

Slowly my friend pulled himself together. He stubbed out his cigarette on the ground beside mine and said in a sullen drawl that was quite unfamiliar to me:

'You know it. And you're the same House as me, and you came two terms earlier. And you're everything I hate. Anything else you want to know?'

Ruprecht was all fists and *furchtbarkeit*. 'We'll add insolence to a monitor to the other charges. And *your* name?'

'Maxwell.'

'House?'

'Chatham.'

'That's a long way from Temple, Maxwell! Is Fernhurst related to you?'

'Not that I know of.'

'All right, you too – insolence to a monitor. You'll both be reported to the headmaster.'

And we were. Fernhurst had his interview first, a two-course meal beginning with a friendly homily on the undesirability of making friends with boys so much younger than himself and ending with six strokes of the cane. He did not speak to me, waiting in the corridor, as he came out.

My ten minutes with J.F. struck me as almost wholly gruesome; the mixture of the understanding man of the world and the cold-blooded executioner was a totally incomprehensible image. (A long room with french windows and standard roses on the lawn outside.) He began by saying in that preposterously self-mocking voice: 'Well, Gavin, what *really* happened?' I repeated everything that had happened as accurately as I could remember it. He said: 'Then you *weren't* smoking when Ruprecht caught you?'

'No, sir, but I had been a few minutes before.'

'Well, Gavin, because you've been so sporting as to tell me that I'm only going to give you two. But before you bend over I want a word with you. It's better, my *dear* fellow, to make

161

friends of your own age and in your own House. It leads to fewer complications. I've told Fernhurst the same. It's not smoking I'm talking about – that's no sin, but it's against school rules, and that's what you're being punished for. Now bend over.'

It hurt like hell, and I never went birds-nesting with Fernhurst again, but I didn't understand why.

So that was the end of Fernhurst – it takes two to make a rendezvous. I began consciously to look for somebody who conformed to J.F.'s prerequisites: in the same House and near the same age. I actually worked it out on paper one evening in prep; there was only one who shared my preoccupation with wild creatures, and he was a year younger than I. He was an athlete, of striking appearance and extremely likeable character, so that he was far from lacking in friends. I began a cold-blooded intellectual wooing, because I needed his company to replace Fernhurst (who had, in the natural course of events and because of his age, left Stowe). To my surprise he responded immediately. John Kent was wholly and wonderfully satisfactory, apparently unaware that he possessed so many qualities that I lacked, unaware that he could command admiration on many levels, unaware that I was proud of his friendship. So the memories of my second and last summer at Stowe are coloured, until the last disastrous day, by recollections of happy unquestioning hours spent in his company by lake and by pasture and by mighty oaks. If these lacked the narrow, penetrating ecstasy of riding Giddy above Beachy Head at St Wulfric's, they were, nevertheless, a broad path of contentment, and their savour lay in at least a partial worship of another human being.

That summer my mother rented a house in the wilder part of Northumberland, not far from Kielder Castle, which was Uncle Alan's grouse-moor near the headwaters of the Tyne. With the house she rented an outlying portion of the moor itself, for by now all three of her sons were enthusiastic shots.

162

This was more like Elrig than any other place I had yet been to, though at the same time I became aware of Northumberland as having a precise flavour of its own, a flavour of which the essence was imparted by distant but intense gleams of sunshine upon a field or a hill, like a spotlight bringing into sudden focus some detail of a huge tapestry.

Besides walking day-long over the Whickhope moor which my mother had rented – an enormous acreage of high heather moor almost devoid of game – we had two days' grouse-driving at Kielder itself. At the beginning of the first day my Uncle Alan drew us aside and gave us a tactful, hesitant talk upon safety rules to be observed by guns using a line of butts. He was embarrassed; and I, though he could not possibly have known or cared, was resentful, because from the ghost of my father I had learnt all there was to know about the theory of every kind of shooting. I had never shot driven grouse before; the strange thing about the day was that I only fired at four and killed them all. However, nobody congratulated me; probably they were too relieved that the rest of the party were still alive to focus attention upon flukes. In the evening I inscribed in my modest Game Book: 'Kielder Castle. Guns: Duke of Northumberland, Lord Percy, Lord Hugh Percy, Lord Morvern Cavendish-Bentinck, Aymer Maxwell, Eustace Maxwell, G.M. 47 grouse, 6 snipe, 1 blackcock, 4 rabbits.' I regret that under 'Remarks' the only entry is: 'G.M. 100 per cent.'

Aunt Victoria spent the summer holidays with us. She had, in late middle age, just learnt to drive a car, and had bought, characteristically, one of the two smallest models existing, a Morris Minor. It was very small and very toy-like, and the coachwork was of brown fabric. Her style of driving was individual. While, for example, other drivers might reverse cautiously out of a garage, head turned over the shoulder, Aunt Victoria would shoot out backwards under full throttle, staring rigidly to her front like a Guardsman on parade. She anthropomorphized her car, so that its occasional mechanical defects appeared to her as character-quirks; and when the foot-throttle jammed open she charged a steep hill with the hand-brake held full on and the admiring comment: 'The little thing's so keen I can hardly hold her back!' Spurr, my mother's very peculiar chauffeur, explained the trouble to her and rectified it, but my aunt said: 'It was nicer to think of it the other way.'

Spurr was one of the most spectacular in the series. He was a very handsome young man in his late twenties, and he brought with him his own uniform, strikingly cut on the lines of a French cavalry officer's; wide, flaring breeches and a tightly waisted tunic. With these stage properties he cultivated, too, the appropriate gestures and mannerisms. In the morning he would appear on the gravel sweep outside the front door, coming to attention with an exaggerated military salute and the clipped words: 'Orders for the day, sir.' His behaviour after dark was less impeccable; he had a girl-friend in Newcastle, many miles distant, and after we were all asleep he would pinch the big Studebaker tourer and spend the night on the tiles. After a time the sound of his coming and going excited comment, not to say wonder, but he countered instantly with the story of a ghost car whose nocturnal antics had frightened him since he first arrived at the house; he had not mentioned it, he explained, for fear of alarming Lady Victoria and the children. When he was finally caught in the act of being the ghost he accepted the situation with complete sangfroid, and left with the same impossibly pretentious salute as he had entered.

12

A CHRISTMAS AND A BIRTHDAY

IN THE CHRISTMAS holidays after my fifteenth birthday we all went to stay with my Aunt and Uncle Northumberland at Alnwick Castle for the Hunt Ball. Of the thirty or forty guests I was by several years the youngest; I was also the only one possessing neither a tail-coat, dinner-jacket, nor the least grain of *savoir-faire*. The *mores* of what is now called Establishment life were as foreign to me as the rules and conventions of my first school had been, for my whole upbringing had represented a secession from precisely this background. Moreover, I was now of an age when the desperate desire to conform and be accepted socially gave rise to greater mental anguish than could ever be known to a ten-year-old. There was no one to instruct me; my brother had little more experience than I, and my mother, though this had been her home, knew only the female side of life, and in Victorian and Edwardian days at that.

Even after all these years I can hardly write of my major gaffe without experiencing again something of the agony it caused me then; thinking of it I shrink to fit that subfusc suit that was my garment of shame; reliving it my heart reaches out with a gush of compassion to all who know the dreadful uncertainties of adolescence, the tormented confusion of social failure. There were three incidents in one evening, and by the third I had become incapable of speech or rational behaviour.

I had a bath before dinner – early, because I was determined that at least I would not be late down to the drawing-room. I dawdled in the bath, because I realized that in my zeal for punctuality I had overdone it, and that I should have more than half an hour to put away. Blissfully unaware that I had left the bathroom door unlocked, I lay in the shallow water with my back to it, idly twirling my pubic hair into two neat little buffalo horns with a parting down the centre. The door opened. Instead of performing any conventional gesture of modesty I scrambled precipitately to my feet and turned to face the sound. I found myself confronting in all my bizarre nudity a very pretty blond girl of about twenty, clothed in an elaborately frilly pink dressing-gown and carrying a bath-towel over her arm. Whereas my own reactions to the situation had been so very inappropriate, hers might have been scripted for her by a ham playwright. She gasped, turned scarlet as her eyes took in my nether coiffure; she said: 'Heavens!' in a steam-engine whisper, and her free hand went up to cover her mouth. Then she was gone with a slam of the door. My very first action, even before locking the door, was comparable to that of a child who has been caught writing something obscene on a blackboard – I rubbed it out. That is to say I seized a towel and scrubbed my bush back to normal, as if it were responsible for the whole incident. Then I spent ten minutes in the bathroom not daring to go back to my room lest I should meet her in the passage. Dressing, I was obsessed by the needling knowledge that there was a girl in the house who knew just what I looked like without any clothes on, and by the idea that she would tell all her friends and giggle about it. It didn't occur to me that it might have been quite a pleasurable experience for her, or that there was nothing unusual or unpleasant about my body.

I found my way to the drawing-room. It was empty, but for an enormous butler who stood in the entrance carrying a silver salver. As I approached him he advanced upon me, proffering the salver in complete silence. My inspection of it was cursory; I did not dare to hesitate and thus display my ignorance. A rapid, furtive glance had shown me that the tray was covered with folded white cards, each standing like two playing-cards propped together as the first stage of a card castle. None of them appeared to have anything written on it. I was clearly required to take one, so I treated it as a sort of lucky-dip; I closed my eyes firmly and took one at random.

The butler showed no surprise, and withdrew. I went on into the drawing-room, and when I was certain that I was alone I cautiously examined what I had taken. On the outside – the side, presumably, that had faced away from me – was written 'Captain George Babington-Smith', and on the inside 'Please take Lady Anne Egerton into dinner.' A tremor of something like giddiness swept over me. The fact that there could be no way of escaping detection did not immediately strike me; as in the bathroom, my first instinct was to expunge the outward and visible sign, and I hurried to throw the evidence into the fire. It was only after I had done so that I began to be racked by guilt. I had made an irreparable muddle; the romance between Captain Babington-Smith and Lady Anne Egerton, of which I knew, would be shattered because of my clumsiness, and I could think of no way of putting things right. I began to rehearse what I might say to him when he came down: 'Captain Babington-Smith', I would say with a charmingly *insouciant* smile, 'I'm terribly sorry but I'm afraid I took your card by mistake,' – but then I realized that by burning the card I had made all explanation impossible. I waited miserably, saying little prayers to myself that what I had done might be undone. Then it occurred to me that because the butler had presented the salver to me there obviously must be somebody whom *I* was supposed to take in to dinner, and I had no means of finding out who it was. I skulked in a distant corner of the drawing-room while the guests congregated; I saw the girl who had come into the bathroom and I edged to keep out of her sight; presently I spotted the couple whom I had sundered, talking cheerfully together as though my prayers had been answered and the Lord had wiped clean the slate of the last half-hour. My ears must have been twitching like a rabbit's, straining for the least word from any quarter that would betray knowledge of my secret. A raddled old lady who cannot have been less than eighty, plastered with makeup, crusted and collared with diamonds, darted a snake-like glance at me and I caught her emery-paper attempt at a whisper. '*Such* an attractive-looking boy, but they say he's *so* shy.'

(Later I repeated this to my sister, omitting the latter half of the sentence and adding: 'I'm going to make a collection of all the nice things that have ever been said about me, and publish it.' She replied: 'And I shall make a collection of all the nasty things that have been said about you, twice as long, and publish that.' I was easily deflated.) Time dragged on; the rest of my family arrived but I shunned them, waiting miserably for the *dénouement* that would come when dinner was announced. It came with the anti-climax of a time-bomb with a dud fuse; the guests went in in pairs, Captain Babington-Smith with Lady Anne Egerton, and I, with no partner, slunk in last.

I sat between two young men in pink coats who talked only with the girls at their other sides. I was grateful for this, but at the same time it seemed yet another indignity that in the seating arrangements I should be treated as a girl and in the event as one unworthy of notice.

My final shame was still to come. Quite early on in the meal my knife slipped on the plate and a large green pea shot into the middle of the table, leaving an irregular spoor of gravy behind it. There it lay, seeming to me as big as a football, while course succeeded course and the footmen ignored it with studious spite. It was still there when they cleared everything else away and brought the dessert-plates; it was still there when the ladies left the room and I was able to move a few places up the table and disown it for ever.

I moved up and sat next to Aymer, who, though I did not guess it, was feeling very nearly as insecure as I was. My uncle, however, did guess it, and with a gesture of kindness which I shall always remember he left his place at the distant head of the table and came all the way down to sit beside us in his resplendent pink coat, and to talk to us as if we were the most important of all his guests. From that moment I didn't care what 'Janitor' thought of him; he joined my heroes, and when he died suddenly, only nine months later, I wished miserably that I had even been able to tell him how grateful I had been.

Among all the works on adolescent psychology that I have read I have not found one whose author seems to remember what it is like to be an adolescent. They state academic truths, but the standpoint is external, as detached as if they were recording experimental data on the behaviour of laboratory rats, and no one can remember what it feels like to be a laboratory rat. The abyss that gapes between the average adult and the average adolescent is not fundamentally a failure of knowledge – though that, too, exists in the great majority of cases – but a failure of understanding that is less excusable, for it is due to a wilful, often compulsive forgetfulness. Pavlov found that he could produce anxiety states in dogs by creating conditions of uncertainty. Most adolescents live in a perpetual state of uncertainty, and therefore of anxiety, because of an immutable attitude in their elders towards what is, for the adolescent, a mutable set of circumstances. The normal adolescent revolt against authority is not, as I see and re-member it, a challenge to the existence of the boss figures – who are more necessary then than they have ever been before – but a protest against their inadequacy, their failure in elas-ticity; in short simply their failure to remember. In particular, their failure to remember that values which have become absolute to them are not so to the adolescent. In adult terms cancer of the brain is of more absolute significance than pimples on the face, future bankruptcy of more absolute im-portance than the present wearing of unsuitable clothes. These concepts are meaningless to the emoting adolescent; the pim-ples and the unsuitable clothes may cause him the greatest amount of disturbance of which he believes himself capable, and they are therefore obstacles in his path as monstrous as cancer or bankruptcy to the adult. If he measured the im-portance of any circumstance or happening he would do so only in measurement units of his own disturbance, not by any absolute standards that are the product of environment and experience.

So the muddle that I had produced that evening seemed to me as great, and the consequences as appalling, as any international crisis can ever have appeared to a statesman whose ineptitude had produced it. True that I didn't actually contemplate suicide, but very few boys do, and I should say even fewer eminent statesmen.

It is always tempting to establish a turning-point in one's life, especially in one's youth, that determines in a wider sense all succeeding events. Such simplifications are suspect, rarely valid, for closer examination usually reveals a character tendency that would in any case have imposed a pattern independent of events. In my case, however, there can be no doubt that my sixteenth birthday began the formative days of my adolescence and thus largely of my adult life, shaping a whole attitude and approach that persisted for many years. For on that day, July 15th, 1930, my hesitant manhood was dragged forcibly back into the prison of invalid childhood and dependence.

I was beginning to emerge, though perhaps almost imperceptibly from an outside standpoint, from my intense shyness and verbal armour; I had just begun to prefer company to solitude, just begun to lose my basic distrust and fear of other boys in the mass. By my friendships with Fernhurst and Kent I had also started to seek mutual interests and background, rather than accepting *ipso facto* the boy at the next desk or in the next bed as a friend because of his proximity. I was, despite a complicated façade, a country boy, familiar with the names and habits of birds and animals and I had found others of the same tastes; a few who, though distrusting my precocious handwriting, my interests in such suspect subjects as poetry and my hypocritical lack of interest in sex, were prepared to accept me in the role of a sort of Mowgli with a gun.

The gun was, I remember, a pistol firing a ·410 shotgun cartridge; I had coveted such a weapon for a long time, and had finally saved the purchase price by various dubious deals in tame jackdaws, Little Owls and the manufacture and sale of an owl-food composed of crushed beetles and meat scraps from the school butcher's shop. The actual possession of the pistol, and the smell of gun oil on the handkerchief in which it was habitually wrapped, represented realized dreams of glory, a whole world outside the form-rooms in which I was bullied for my day-dreaming. Inside strictly school confines my sense of inadequacy reduced me to inanity or hypocrisy, using my tongue as a flail, I now realize, to protect mental and physical virginity from outrage.

On this Saturday, July 15th, my mother and my eldest brother Aymer, by then at Cambridge, were to come to take me out to lunch; but I had planned an earlier entertainment than this. I had arranged with another boy in my dormitory to climb out of the house at dawn and go rabbit shooting until breakfast-time. Each of us had persuaded the boy in the next bed to demolish at the right moment the pillow-dummy that we would leave under the sheets, and we would go straight from our rabbit shoot to the pre-breakfast roll-call in Assembly.

A dull grey dawn with the dew sopping on deep summer grass and nettles. Everything smelled wet and green, and the air was intimate with the calling of jackdaws awakening from their hollow oaks and Palladian ruins. A sense of adventure and liberation; in all the world we were the only two awake, the only two hunters. Pale wet sheets of mist lay flat over the lakes, and from the reed-beds at their edges came voices of mallard and coot. The whole crowded, organized world of school dissolved into this daybreak that seemed primordial and without context. A dinosaur emerging from the reeds of the Octogan Lake would have been less anachronistic than the sudden appearance of, say, my Latin form master with his city suit, shiny pointed black shoes, rimless lenses and mincing accent. I was the young predator in the dim red dawn of man – or perhaps more appropriately a small tortoise sticking its neck out with an absorbing sense of discovery, only to have that head chopped off before twenty-four hours had passed.

We crawled through long drenching grass to the edge of a

sandpit rabbit-warren. Questing rabbits' ears and nostrils, the thump of a hind foot and the flash of a white scut. I shot a young rabbit, adolescent and adventuresome as we were, and passed the pistol to my companion, and he waited for the slow recovery of confidence in the warren. The coneys are a foolish folk; he had only to wait for five minutes. During that time he was lying to my right and a little in front of me. I looked at his profile, at his ears, at the down at the corner of his lips. I remember thinking: 'You're *ugly* – much uglier than the rabbit,' and an odd feeling of disappointment crept over me, disappointment that my companion of the moment was coarse in feature and in form, not the faun who should share this moment in which I rediscovered a host of earlier certainties. Suddenly I thought of Heisch at Heddon Court, and of Craith.

A nose and ears appeared at the entrance to a burrow, tentative, questioning; the whole contents of the little cartridge hit the young rabbit in the face, and he lay at the entrance to his home, purple-blooded and mashed. I said to myself again: 'He's uglier than the rabbit.' It was an enormous satisfaction to me to discover that the other boy did not know how to gut a rabbit. I showed him, expertly and with contempt. (A sheath-knife with a roe-horn handle. It was one of my favourite possessions, and I never saw it after that day.)

While I was gutting the rabbits it began to rain. At first there were a few very heavy drops, falling straight and squashy from a big dark cloud; then the volume increased until it was tropical, obliterating. We were nearly a quarter of a mile from the nearest Palladian folly that might shelter us; we ran, but by the time we had reached it we were as wet as if we had been bathing fully clothed. The other boy complained, and I put on a cave-boy act, saying that I never noticed whether clothes were wet or dry. He was irritated, and began to read the *graffiti* on the walls of the little temple. As in all the follies at that time there were drawings, assignations and curiously erudite obscenities in Latin and Greek. Here someone had superimposed upon these a sentence of big roman capitals:

172

'Samples of the whitewash from these walls have been taken for comparative analysis with those from dormitories, and when identification is certain J.F. will personally congratulate all contributors.' As always, I was embarrassed by the evidence of a clamouring world of sex of which I understood so little, a world from which I felt myself obscurely debarred despite the promptings of my body. So when my companion began to talk sex I shut him up with an aloof display of sophistication that was pathetically far from the truth.

The rain kept on falling in a steady deluge, and when at last it stopped we only had twenty minutes left to get to Assembly. If it had gone on raining there would have been other wet boys among whom to hide ourselves; now we should be conspicuous unless there was another shower. Our pre-arranged plans had fallen to pieces. Now we decided to bank upon other boys from our detached House crossing to the main building with mackintoshes; each of us would approach Chatham from different directions, get mackintoshes to cover our sodden grey suits, and make for Assembly. We concealed the rabbits and the pistol, and separated.

Boys were just beginning to leave the House when I reached it. A few drops of rain were falling again and nearly everyone was wearing or carrying a mackintosh. I dived into the house for mine and literally bumped into my under-housemaster. I stood awkward and blushing, finding nothing to say, while he gave me that long searching, disquieting look whose meaning I had yet to learn. Boys jostled past us, some running. At last I said something like, 'Sir, I must go to Assembly,' and made to move. He put out his hand and stopped me, slipping the palm under the shoulder of my jacket and on to the waterlogged shirt. 'You're very wet,' he said, looking very hard at me with his bright blue eyes. 'It's your birthday, isn't it? Go to Assembly without a mack – it's raining again. And run. Change after breakfast before chapel – I'll tell Matron.' Then, as I turned to leave him, 'By the way, were you alone?' Instinctively I said, 'Yes, sir,' and instinctively I knew, without formulating the idea of adult emotion, that the question was

173

not put from disciplinarian motives. I ran, and he called after me, 'Many happy returns of the day.' It was nearly twenty years before I saw him again.

I passed the morning's school in no more and no less of a dream than usual; in fact I think my thoughts were more than ordinarily focused, for I was wondering whether the pistol would get rusty before I could get to it in the evening. My mother and Aymer would arrive soon after midday, and I felt it as necessary to conceal my escapade from them as, for example, not to mention a note that I had been passed at breakfast, 'Sweet sixteen and never been —.' My brother, at the age of eighteen, seemed to me a very mature man of the world. By one of those swift changes of role that characterized our childhood he was no longer, when he visited me at school, the constant companion of the holidays, but a little remote and patronizing, recalling something of the twelve-year-old who at Heddon Court had called me Maxwell minimus. Now when he and my mother came together to see me at school I felt I could have established immediate *rapport* with one or the other, but that I could not cross the two bridges simultaneously.

It was more than ever difficult for me that day, because I was feeling vaguely unwell, a sensation of mental and physical depression that I could not have defined. I was relieved rather than otherwise when they left in the late afternoon. I went to fetch the pistol and the rabbits. These I sold for 6d. each to a boy who had a tame Barn Owl, then I cleaned the pistol and went to the changing-room to change my socks. I remember them, what they looked like when they were on and when they were off, because when I had put them on that morning they had been criticized with exactly that degree of irony that hurt me most. An eighteen-year-old dandy who had caught my wandering attention because when clothed in nothing else he was revealed as possessing a dense pelt of fair curly hair from head to foot, had said: 'Of course, Maxwell, those socks with round zebra stripes look so *smart* with a suit and black shoes, don't they?' ('I didn't buy them, MacLean.' 'Then tell who-ever did.')

I was all alone in the changing-room, and had taken off one sock, when life came to a dead stop. I looked at my foot and thought in a dull repetitive way: 'It can't be mine.' I took off the other sock and I said the Lord's Prayer to myself and then my baby prayer, over and over again. I was scared of someone coming in and finding me like this; in my mind what I saw was somehow equated with the birthmarks on my right fore-arm, something shameful that couldn't be explained away.

Both my feet and ankles were covered with dark purple spots, in some places patches; one pressed them and they did not change or disappear. The joints were swollen, and under pressure they were painful in a dull, aching way. I felt frightened and alone, and without any process of articulation I connected this catastrophe with my morning's escapade, with killing, with sex, somehow with my under-housemaster.

In times of extreme distress I have all my life wanted to be alone, and I can recognize and understand the common pattern between that far-distant day of agonized adolescence and the crises of adult life. Just to be left alone, to recognize, to become something different.

At that moment two boys came in to have a shower, and I fumbled miserably to get my socks back on again before they should see anything. They were not paying any attention to me; they were betting on the sizes of their waists. I remember the tableau as I turned to go, because it was the very last image of ordinary schoolboy life that I was ever part of. They had stripped, and the elder standing on a bench below the coat-hangers had collapsed his diaphragm while the other drew a snake belt tight round it. And tighter, and tighter. The elder gasped: 'That hurts – let me go.' The younger tried, but the belt got stuck and he became frightened. 'For Christ's sake, Maxwell, come and help – David's going to choke!' David stood as though crucified, with his arms up and resting on two coat-hangers, a mass of straight ash-blond hair fallen forward over his face. I got the belt off with difficulty. He remained in

175

the same attitude, breathing deeply; then he said: 'Thanks, Maxwell.' Then, suddenly: 'What's wrong with your ankle?'

He was standing on a bench, and to reach the belt I had put one foot on it. The sock had slipped down, and now revealed an inch or two of those dreadful purple spots.

I was nearly in tears when I told him. He was kindly and sensible, though he was younger than I. 'It looks so odd it might be something serious,' he said. 'You ought to go to Matron at once.'

Alnwick Castle

So I went. She was always kind, paedophile, but now she was puzzled; this was outside her training. She said: 'Have you been eating strawberries?' I said no. (They had been finished by the time we had arrived for a late lunch at Brackley.) She took my temperature and said: 'How do you feel? Just how do you feel ill?' She wanted to be kind, and I sensed it, but I couldn't answer. 'Just ill,' I said, 'something's wrong.' I wanted reassurance; I asked: 'It's not serious, is it Matron? I'm not really ill?' and she replied: 'To be honest I don't know. You must go to the San, and Dr Bostock will say.'

So I went, with my pyjamas and sponge-bag, to the sanatorium. When I left, I passed the whole school going into chapel, but I was no longer part of anything but my own fears and the curious dull pain that seemed gradually to be invading my whole body.

I was put to bed in a room by myself. There was a bowl of flowers – I think they were white chrysanthemums. It seemed a very long time before the doctor came, and by that time the pain had taken over my stomach besides all my joints. He asked me: 'Are there any "bleeders" in your family?' and because I connected this word vaguely with menstruation I became confused and could not answer. Later, my brother came back, but by then I was feeling too terribly ill even to seek reassurance. In the morning I was taken by ambulance to a nursing-home in Weybridge; of the journey I remember only darkness and pain and the sudden sweet release of morphia.

13

SNOWFALL IN SUMMER

'Gavin Maxwell, aged 16.0 years, was admitted to St Theresa's nursing-home, Weybridge, on July 16th, 1930, suffering from Henoch's purpura of unknown aetiology. The condition showed certain characteristics of Purpura haemorrhagica, as in addition to extensive ecchymosis there was varying haemorrhage from all mucous surfaces and massive excretion of blood from bladder and bowel. On first examination the patient was in great pain and had already received maximal sedation. After dangerous prostration and repeated transfusion, crisis was passed on August 5th, and he made satisfactory progress until his discharge from the nursing-home on August 23rd, 1930. . . .'

At first I was conscious for very little of the time, and of that little I should remember even less if I had not tried to write of it not long afterwards. Existence as I was aware of it was an alternating sequence of pain, morphia, pain, morphia; the pain, fierce and consuming as I bled internally, is associated with a dull red haze in front of my eyes; the morphia changed the red to a translucent white mist on which, disembodied, I floated with an infinite contentment towards what became a known and certain destination – Elrig in the spring. Sometimes I reached it, looking down from a height upon the grey house on the hill-side, the blowing daffodils and the budding elms of the rookery, and more than once in the moment of transition to consciousness and pain I was looking down upon my own sickbed in the half-light of the curtained room, seeing the ever-present nurse and my mother sitting one on either side of the bed.

As my condition worsened and I sank towards the crisis, my moments of consciousness and clarity became fewer; and in them, besides the pain, I suffered agonies of thirst which I was not allowed to quench. I knew where I wanted to drink from, a small stream at Elrig, where the water ran shallow over small pebbles, and in my mind I would lie prone at its bank and part the overhanging heather to bury my face in the sweet chill of its flow. I remember one night when what was left of my conscious mind decided quite coldly to die out of spite; I had returned in the small hours to the confusion of physical misery which was the only waking world I now knew, and the nurse refused me morphia, saying that it was the doctor's orders that I should have no more. I remember her face, an ugly, blotchy pug face with bunches of red hair showing round her nurse's head-dress. I turned my face away from her and tried to die and found that I couldn't, and began to cry in a desolation of self-pity. Only in the morning was I allowed more morphia, and then it was in too small a dose to carry me to Elrig on my cloud. That day my mother told me that one of the greatest doctors in the world was coming to see me, and in the evening Lord Horder, physician to the King, was ushered into the room with a degree of deference that penetrated even my dimmed perceptions. He was short and dark and very formally dressed, and I disliked him on what little sight I had. I remember him looking down at me and slowly shaking his head from side to side. It was like a judge putting on the black cap, but I think I was too far gone to care, because I did not feel afraid. Then he picked up my right arm as it lay outside the bedclothes, and said to my own doctor: 'Should you come across this condition again, Doctor, it is worth noting that these ecchymoses on the right forearm are diagnostically perhaps the most typical.'

There was very little by then that could have roused me into the intense effort of speech; I did not understand the word 'ecchymoses', but I understood that he was pointing to my birth-marks; and this, because I had been for so long and deeply ashamed of them, stung me in a way that I could not have explained. I tried to say something, but the words wouldn't come out properly. He bent over me and asked:

'What did you say?' I spent a moment gathering together
the strength I had; then I managed to say in a perfectly cle
and normal voice that held a venom that I could hear mysel
'Those are birth-marks, you bloody fool!' I saw him blus
which was the only active pleasure I had known for a lor
time, and my mother, who had never heard me swear in h
life, said 'Gavin!' with a note of shocked reproof, but a secon
afterwards I saw the corners of her mouth twitch; it must hav
been the nearest she had come to genuine amusement fo
weeks. A long time later she told me that Lord Horder, wh
had chanced to be dining within a few hundred yards of th
nursing-home, had charged fifty guineas for this consultatio
He did not tell my mother in so many words that I was goin
to die, but that my chances of survival were very slende
Perhaps it was because of this that I was allowed, that nigh
enough morphia to carry me to Elrig again, but I saw it a
from a greater height, seeing the moorlands stretch awa
beyond it to the waste-lands of heather where the Drumwa
Lochs shone with a bright enamel blue and there were sea
birds wheeling in the air around me.

The next morning my mother told me that Mr Rees ha
come to see me. Mr Rees was a minister of our Church, and i
was only then that I understood clearly that everyone though
I was going to die. He came into the twilit room, and withou
speaking to me vested himself in chasuble and stole; then h
unpacked a small Gladstone bag, laid a linen cloth upon
table and set out upon it the miniature Communion plate tha
is used upon such occasions. Then he was by the bedside, an
my mother propped me up a very little to receive the Las
Sacrament. The minister's tired old voice began the words
knew so well. 'The body of our Lord Jesus Christ, broken fo
thee, preserve thy body and soul unto everlasting life,' and he
placed a tiny fragment of the wafer between my lips. 'The
blood of our Lord Jesus Christ, shed for thee . . .' and a single
drop of the Communion wine passed between my lips before
the cup was withdrawn and my mother lowered me to the
pillow again. From this ritual I received, because of my up-

180

bringing, a true and unquestioning comfort, and as the minister's voice murmured on: 'The peace of God that passeth all understanding keep your heart and mind. . . .' I was as relaxed as a subject under hypnosis. When Mr Rees had gone my mother came back into the room and sat down beside the bed. I whispered to her: 'Mother, am I going to die?' She answered: 'Only if God wants you,' and I could see that her eyes were full of tears. If I had died then it would have been peacefully and without a struggle; I thought about it, and felt that it would be like the morphia, that I should float away through space and time to Elrig in perpetual spring sunshine.

Of the slow climb from that nadir I remember very much less than of the days of descent. The bleeding stopped, pain became less and then altogether absent; the curtains were drawn back and I found that my bed was in a large ground-floor room with french windows opening on to a lawn bordered with wallflowers and snapdragons. I began to resent the in-dignities of my helplessness, the shame of rectal feeding, enemas and bed-baths, and though I believe I never expressed this resentment it became a deep-seated part of my attitude; I felt that I was being refused permission to grow up and become independent. A host of women were about my bed and my bath and spying out all my ways; I yearned for male com-panionship, so that even the least inspiring school company now seemed infinitely desirable, the physical activity of one of those miserable Stowe runs in winter preferable to the utter immobility now imposed upon me. This was more than a figure of speech, for it was the belief of those in charge of me that any movement might bring a recurrence of the bleeding; I sat in bed propped up by pillows, and in my right hand was a push-button bell which I must sound for anything I wanted, even though it might be within easy hand's reach.

Because of this it was very difficult to pass the time; I could read from a book on a book-rest, but I was not allowed to turn the pages for myself, nor could I write, draw, do jigsaw-puzzles, or any of the other common pastimes of the convalescent. It was long before the days of television, and as far as I can remember I had no radio. My mother would read aloud to me for hours, but in the past I had always been used to draw or paint while she did this, and I felt bitterly un-fulfilled. Through the french windows on to the lawn I watched everything that was free – glossy starlings hurrying about the lawn and prodding it with their open beaks, chirping sparrows in short, rapid flight between the grass and the virginia creeper on the walls, butterflies lilting aimlessly above the flower borders – and envied them and day-dreamed. Once, through those windows, I saw a flightless young sparrow killed by a white cat, and I identified myself so completely with the victim that I cried with rage and frustration. All the nebulous longings of adolescence were canalized for me into the one master desire for physical freedom, to walk ten miles, to climb trees, to sprint, even to submit to any of the physical duresses that I had hated.

This state of mind became intensified during the mild inebriation that my daily diet dictated. I had to drink half a bottle of champagne every day; I hated it, as I had always disliked all fizzy drinks, but despite the accompanying nausea the effort lowered my threshold to a world of fantasy in which I was once again a boy with the full use of his limbs and as free of adult control as any of my known contemporaries. Some-times this image would become more precise; I would be my elder brother Aymer, eighteen years old, emancipated, hand-some, with a fast car of his own and the world at his feet. Or I would be John Kent, younger than I, but with his athlete's grace and freedom of movement, with the gentle self-assurance that his physical prowess and his looks gave him as birthright. I spent a long time being him, after he wrote to me quite unexpectedly – the only person outside my family who did so while I was in the nursing-home. I remember the letter-heading, and the careful upright handwriting expressing a thought strangely mature for a fifteen-year-old. He had been told of the progress of my illness by my under-housemaster.

I can still remember much of John's letter. 'I'm told that

you mayn't [the apostrophe was in the wrong place, after the t] be able to do things like climbing trees and so on again, but don't worry, the idea is more important than doing it and this applies to most things doesn't it. If you don't come back to Stowe would you like to come and stay here for part of a holidays? I saw 22 Canada geese near Bucklow mere yesterday. . . .' So then for a few days I was John, winning every athletic contest, seeing Canada geese instead of starlings and sparrows, asking my friends to stay.

All my family came to visit me, Aymer, Eustace, Christian, and my Percy aunts and uncles. But in the approach of my brothers and sister I sensed an embarrassment towards, almost a refusal to accept a responsibility for, this new situation; in the past they might have subconsciously desired subordination, but this overt helplessness and utter dependence was more than any of them had bargained for.

For the first three weeks of my illness I had known nothing beyond my little enclosed world of twilight and pain, and I had never speculated on where my mother was living or how she came and went. She could not drive a car (she did not learn until after her sixtieth birthday, early in the Second World War) and for the first time she had no chauffeur. In fact her family were ferrying her, and sometimes by very unconventional transport. Eustace's motor cycle, for example.

Eustace, having acquired the money to buy a motor cycle, characteristically bought the largest one he could find. (It is strange to think that in those days there was no test to pass, and that any boy of sixteen who had the necessary money could arm himself with a really lethal weapon.) He then sent this monster to the manufacturers of a spectacular torpedo-shaped sidecar made of stretched fabric over wood, and ordered one to be fitted. This firm was in North London, and Eustace had arranged to collect my mother and take her down to Weybridge on the same afternoon as the work was completed. When he arrived to take the motor cycle away the whole crew of the workshop assembled to see him off. 'You have ridden a combination with a heavy bike before, haven't you?' asked the foreman, and Eustace said airily: 'Oh, hundreds,' although in fact he had never ridden any combination at all, and indeed could hardly ride the motor cycle without the sidecar. He climbed into the saddle, and somehow managed to start the engine despite his inexperience. Under the eyes of all the workshop staff he set off down the road, and in a few yards he discovered what experts refer to as the handling characteristics of the vehicle. In another few, with a splintering crash, he had rammed the shiny bullet nose of the sidecar into the back of a stationary lorry. He heard cries of dismay behind him, and looking in the mirror he could see the whole staff pelting down the pavement towards him. Unwilling to accept either their sympathy or their ridicule, he extricated himself with frantic speed and was once again under unsteady way while they were still ten yards behind.

It might have been during the time that I was very ill indeed, for my mother was so distraught that she did not even notice that when she climbed into the sidecar her feet were sticking out at the front end.

Early in September I was moved from the nursing-home to the Surrey house, Northfield, on the outskirts of Albury village, that had been my family's winter home for some years. Proximity to one of the Irvingite churches had always been a *sine qua non* to any adherent of the faith, and around the Apostles' Chapel at Albury, on the estate owned by my Uncle Alan Northumberland, there had grown up a veritable colony of the sect, of whom the greater number in Albury were spinsters. The heart of that dreaming valley, in those days, was the curious, isolated Irvingite church, certainly not without a certain bizarre rural beauty; I know too little of church architecture, despite my mother's early and patient attempts at education, to define it. In my parlance of those days I probably could not have got further than saying that it stood alone, at the end of a hundred-yard drive from the road, among chestnut trees, and that it seemed a series of pale yellow spires

184

encrusted with small bobbles. There, and there only, we met our neighbours on Sundays, before or after services, in the brief minutes between exodus from the church and entry into our cars parked in the space below the church steps, or before the other members of the congregation started home on foot.

The full and proper name of our house was Lower North-field, whose qualifying adjective seemed to me in my child-hood snobbism, to be a slight; it was a modest house on the lane leading past the parish church, separated from Upper Northfield by a yew hedge, and we shared it with my Aunt Victoria, who, on the field sloping down from it to the road and the stream in the valley below, had created her vast Chinchilla rabbit fur farm. There I was installed, still at first almost immobile, in what had been the principal bedroom on the first floor. The window looked on to the lawn enclosed by high yew hedges; other starlings, as busy and beautiful as those of the nursing-home, scurried and jabbed at its smooth turf; my aunt's black-and-white nun pigeons whickered past my window and drank at the bird-table or crooned in the eaves, symbols of freedom each and every one of them.

Gradually I was allowed a little movement, first enough to turn the pages of my own book, then to write and to draw, and at last to have a bath – though I was not allowed to dry myself after it. For a time my earlier frustrations became latent, and despite isolated spells of self-pity I became resigned to a life that was at least secure and free from physical discomfort. More, in a curious negative sense it was luxurious. I was waited upon for my smallest fulfillable desire; I had come to like the champagne that I had so detested in the nursing-home, and my food, though limited in scope was exquisitely cooked. I remember it as almost invariable, though I never grew weary of it; sole, in crisp golden brown *goujons*, in firm white steamed cones down which the melted butter trickled as down a spiral staircase, and sole in fish soufflés and casseroles, sole grilled and fried and steamed and boiled – and with it the only substitute I was allowed for salt, Marmite. I imagine that my kidneys must have been affected by my illness, for I was forbidden any form of mineral salt, and in the craving that the human body has for salt in any form I would lick clean whole jars of Marmite and use a teaspoonful to every *goujon* of sole. With such minor pleasures of the body, and infinite leisure to read, to draw, to paint and to write, I became as superficially contented as any potentially active invalid of sixteen can be. Of fiercer physical delights I still knew nothing for some weeks to come.

Soon after I was moved from the nursing-home to the best bedroom at Northfield, my Uncle Alan Northumberland died. It was in September, and I remember that it was a rainy grey morning, because it was the weather that caused my gaucherie. During my last year at Stowe I had had a dog, an un-manageable liver-and-white Springer Spaniel with light yel-low eyes, and he was now boarded with Uncle Alan's game-keeper at Albury Park, half a mile away. My mother had promised that the gamekeeper Powell should bring Tracker over to see me on the first dry day – this so that he should not spread mud and water all over the sick-room. The day before had been sunny and dry, and I had pestered my mother to be allowed to see Tracker, but she had been preoccupied and busy, and said that the weather would be just as fine to-morrow. So when I woke in the morning and saw the rain teeming down on the lawn and dripping past the window from the creepers I was almost in tears of frustration. My world had contracted to a very small compass, and these trivialities seemed to me of vital importance. When my mother came into the room I began immediately upon petulant reproach, but I stopped, horrified, when I saw that she was sobbing, for she always displayed the greatest self-control in the presence of her children. My uncle had died early that morning, of a per-forated duodenal ulcer.

I thought about him all that day and for some days after; most of all I remembered his spontaneous kindliness the previous winter, when he had left the head of the great table and by-passed his host of dazzling guests to come down and comfort two schoolboys paralysed by shyness. I felt again the warm outflowing of affection that I had felt towards him then, and I felt genuine grief that I had never been able to communicate it to him. But I also remember, as time went on, an entirely different and mean little emotion, a nasty and utterly egocentric little thought that I tried to suppress and couldn't. Uncle Alan had been my only godfather. At my christening, after the outbreak of war, he had at my mother's request given me an austerity christening-present; instead of a silver mug I had received a horn mug and a horn spoon. After that, with four years of war to erase immediate recollection of such small matters, the fact that he was my godfather had passed clean out of his mind, so that the various occasional largesse dealt out to my brothers and sister by their sponsors never came my way. Only a year before his death he was somehow reminded that he was in fact my godfather and that I was now fifteen years old, and he had at once begun spectacularly to make up for previous omissions. His first gesture by way of reparation had been to present me with a gun, an expensive Hardy split-cane trout rod, a full set of golf-clubs and a cash present – all this, I fancy, in face of expostulation from my mother, who always felt that lavish presents tended to spoil. My uncle had also told me with an uncondescending charm that he was ashamed of having forgotten his responsibilities for so long, and that for anything I wanted in the future I might look to him. Now the source of all this magnanimity was gone, and though I knew intellectually that this was a disgusting thought to intrude upon sadness at the death of someone for whom I had felt a short though real affection, it came back to whisper at me accusations of hypocrisy.

At this time what seemed to be a new and much warmer relationship grew between my sister and myself. We revived our nursery jokes and made new ones, played endless games of chess and cards, drew and painted together, and she took great trouble to make me content in my captivity. At that time my reading matter was largely dictated by her – I read, that is to say, whatever she happened to be reading and quoting at the time. Siegfried Sassoon came first, *Memoirs of an Infantry Officer*, *Memoirs of a Foxhunting Man*, and all the war poems; in a week or two I could write exactly like Siegfried Sassoon, and I thought that was admirable. Then she produced Housman's poems, which seemed made to measure for me, and very soon I knew them all, every single one, by heart. Then I found I could write exactly like Housman, and that seemed laudable to me too. In what I conceived to be his manner I wrote a poem about my illness which seemed to me to be fine, and wholly justifiable that I should advance my age by one year for the sake of scansion.

> *When I was seventeen and sick*
> *I prayed that I should die,*
> *As Trinity to Trinity,*
> *My body, soul and I.*
>
> *One stab I felt and fast I fled*
> *From pain and blood and rumpled bed,*
> *And thought the prayer that I had said*
> *Had made me dead.*
>
> *I saw no saints and angels*
> *I heard no trumpets' riot,*
> *For there was nothing left at all*
> *But only conscious quiet.*
>
> *When I was seventeen and sick*
> *And turned me to the wall*
> *'Twas but a hypodermic prick*
> *And morphia after all.*

The concept of trying to write exactly like myself never occurred to me, because, like most adolescents, I had no idea who I was. Next came *The Seven Pillars of Wisdom* and a good deal of Gertrude Bell; Omar Khayyám (also learnt by heart from beginning to end) and *The City of Dreadful Night*.

The undigested fusion of these, together, evidently, with some profound guilt complex, produced poems of appalling sentimentality and woolliness, of which I still remember one, because a little later it was discovered and I was mocked for it and was ashamed. I am not now; it is as stupid to be ashamed of adolescence as to be goaded by the taunt that Rimbaud produced his finest work at sixteen. Few people, and most certainly not I, have had either Rimbaud's genius or his stimuli to precocity; I was groping in a haze of romantic nostalgia.

> I've had enough of wrong and right
> And which is which in others' sight,
> So now my friends I'll say goodnight
> And keep an older law.
>
> To this and that with aching heart
> I've turned but still remained apart,
> So now where fishes poise and dart
> I'll slumber far from shore.
>
> I'm going where the water's deep
> And wrecks have sunk before,
> And there I'll lay me down and sleep
> And be reviled no more.
>
> While I my weary vigil keep
> With nothing but the waves' wild song
> To soothe and hush my fevered sleep
> Still men will talk of right and wrong.
>
> And live and laugh and love and breed,
> Discuss the ethics of some creed,
> They never understood; indeed
> I'm glad that I sleep long.

It was sound and sonority that drew me, and the more melancholy and despairing the better; anything possessing these qualities was good enough for an ear whose critical faculty was entirely undeveloped. My mother had her own personal anthology, copied in longhand into a leather manuscript book, but of those I remember only her favourite poem 'Cold in the snow and fifteen wild Decembers', of which she would say that she disapproved of the sentiments but was intoxicated by the metre, and some unpublished verse by a contemporary on the theme of 'The Charge of the Light Brigade'. For her, too, sonority and the musical quality of verse were all-important, but to her melancholy was suspect, a subject for ridicule, and she preferred her poems to be upon heroic or religious themes.

My reading matter was in fact, strongly censored; no book that might be 'unsuitable' could gate-crash my sick-room, and unsuitability included anything that questioned any part of the established order, and any possible direct or indirect reference to sex. Even when I was well enough, later that autumn, to make brief excursions to Guildford in the car I was not allowed to have my own subscription to a library; I would browse among the shelves with my mother, and if she approved of what I chose I took it out on her subscription. All unaware of my utter ignorance of sexual matters she was afraid, as she told me many years later, that with so little other outlet for my energies I must be obsessed with sex, and like the authors of *What a Young Boy Ought to Know* she believed boyhood masturbation to be exceedingly harmful to health.

I was sixteen and two months, after three years of repressed sexual maturity, before I discovered the secret that I had so long guarded from myself. In the bath, innocent, washing; an obliterating spasm so exquisite that I actually lost consciousness; the colours of the spectrum spinning faster and faster until they became a fierce white ecstasy. A moment later, awareness regained, I was trembling in the witch-doctor's world of my indoctrination; *What a Young Boy Ought to Know*, the pipe-smelling talks – madness, sin and fear, fear, fear. 'Oh Lamb of God that takest away the sins of the world, have mercy upon me. Never, never again – I swear it Jesus.'

And the next day, 'I've failed, I've failed. Oh Lamb of God that takest away the sins of the world, hear my prayer.' Because my inhibitions had lasted so much longer than other boys', they had grown until they were a massive part of me, and their destruction was a drawn-out agony of confusion that could be shared with no one. It was years before I read and accepted a sentence from a medical journal: 'Any attempt to regulate an individual's desired frequency of orgasm is a direct interference with the needs of the whole organism.' An 'attempt to regulate' was a pathetically thin phrase to describe my dreadful Laocoön struggles to kill the phantom serpent; and, because I was incapable of assimilating the idea that other people must have the same instincts with the same intensity, I felt that I was Siamese twin to some demon, a demon that was dragging me down first to madness and then to hell. Thus to the normal adolescent search for identity – the confused desire to find out who one really is, leading to imitation, identification with another, rapid transference of loyalties, disappointment and the withdrawal into oneself so often classified by adults as 'moodiness' – was added the blurred concept of having a split personality in the Jekyll and Hyde sense.

The demon, of course, always won, so that by repeated defeat my other self lost stature steadily in my own eyes. It could recover only by some triumphant assertion of itself, and I am sure that if I had not been an invalid I should at once have become a pre-eminently successful athlete – I should have had a target of acceptable physical prowess and, however over-ambitious, I should have achieved it. I saw the conquest of externals, the winning of prestige, to be the goal, rather than the integration of my own personality, because if I could have put it into words most of what made up my entity I felt to be unacceptable to me or anyone else. Instead, I came to hate my body, feeling that it had betrayed me in every way, and having given the dog a bad name I was ready – but fearful – to impute to it fresh weaknesses and inadequacies in every hour of the twenty-four. An itch at the back of the neck became, by hypothesis, an infection of ringworm; a brief appearance of pimples on the chin was there that the prophecy might be fulfilled, further evidence of the demon's conquest; the least hint of dislike or off-handedness on the part of another was proof that the eyes were the windows of the soul and that mine were muddy.

However the manifestations of sex are viewed by the adolescent, whether with delight or dismay, free-hearted enjoyment or bewilderment and fear, emotional involvement or lonely preoccupation, I believe that they always become the centre-point of life, responsible for all action and underlying motive, a single dominant factor for which there is no earlier parallel. Physically, the change is responsible for a host of gaucheries and gaffes, ranging from aggression, unco-ordinated clumsiness because the body's owner feels its changes to be comic to grown-ups, to moments embarrassing even to an adult with hardly-learned *savoir-faire*. I remember situations to which there just wasn't any answer; being asked, for example, to jump up and open the door for a departing guest at a moment when my serpent, quite forgotten, had taken control of the situation and I couldn't stand up without making this obvious. So one bounded for the door and probably either knocked something over or tripped over something and fell over oneself, and became tongue-tied and puce and miserable for hours afterwards. Or being told to stand up in a class and answer a question at a moment when concealing the same circumstance made concentration impossible. I used to think that these occasions were unique to me, and it was years before I discovered that this particular embarrassment was part of everyone's experience and had been shared by those whom I had thought totally immune.

Discovery of pleasure – what a wholly inadequate word for those ecstasies – came only a few weeks before full intellectual knowledge of what this was all about. My doctor recommended ultra-violet ray therapy, a comparative innovation in those days, and for this purpose I went three times a week to a near-by village where the chemist's wife was a masseuse and midwife. Left alone to dress and undress between appearances in a minimum *cache-sexe*, I discovered a whole library of anatomy and function including Van de Velde's *Ideal Marriage*. Dressing and undressing took a long time. My first reaction was, 'All this says it's *meant* to be pleasurable – even tells you how to get the most pleasure from it'; and then, since it was all about marriage, and nobody I knew married before their twenties, 'What am I supposed to do with this demon body in the next ten years or so?' Everything I could do must be both sin and lead to damnation, or destructive to my body and brain. I thought a lot about it, not always (though often) with lust or prurience, and I remember the precise moment, affixing Guatemalan stamps (plumed birds against a tropical forest background) into a loose-leaf stamp-book, at which the question became real. Dr Vaughan-Evans had said: 'You came here to learn to think. Use your brains on everything you're ever told.' Well, I would use my brains on this. Separating sin and physical harm, how could it hurt my health if it didn't do so after one was married? It couldn't be a question of age, because I had read that one could marry legally at sixteen, so what could it be a question of? There was simply nobody whom I felt I could ask; I was on formal terms with the doctor, whose visits were now less frequent, and the rest of my household consisted of my mother, my Aunt Victoria and my sister. Eustace was at Sandhurst and Aymer at Cambridge – I considered asking him when he came home at Christmas, but as we had never mentioned such things, despite our long alliance, I never brought myself to do so. I made up my mind that boys were told lies about the physical harm so as to stop them sinning, and so the next intellectual target became to discover why it was claimed to be a sin, and for that I turned to the Bible. Exhaustive research yielded nothing from the New Testament; at last, by use of dictionary and concordance, I discovered Onan and how God had killed him for what he had done. But it was clear to me, with the fairly comprehensive theoretical knowledge of sexual activities that I now possessed, that what Onan did had nothing at all to do with me; and moreover that it was not what he did with his seed that worried anyone, but his refusal to have children by his brother's wife – a refusal which would surely have appeared most laudable to my family. So I satisfied myself that this was neither a sin nor in any way harmful; but these decisions, though defiant, left my sense of guilt surprisingly intact.

A few months' later I fell in love, blindingly, hopelessly, with a girl of my own age. Still a semi-invalid, I spent a fortnight with my mother in a friend's house, and at the end of twenty-four hours I was in a world of emotional sensations as utterly new and unforeseen as had been my discovery of physical pleasure. It was the more confusing because I could not have said what I wanted of her; the longing, ocean-deep, poignant as a weeping violin, was supremely unconscious of its purpose. I see her in fragility and a sort of gazelle-like beauty, long-limbed and golden-haired, inturned and secretive as I was myself, against a background contrived for romantic passion. A great drawing-room in which stood a giant potted azalea, white and seven feet high, petals falling upon an Aubusson carpet, the scent of carnations and the sweet chime of a Chelsea eighteenth-century china clock on the chimney-piece, scent and sound fused into identity. A vast chandelier, whose pendants glittered like the 'shinkly' sea of my child-hood. A grand piano, on which she played and sang 'Pale hands I loved beside the Shalimar – where are you now?' Well, where are you now? Not beside the Shalimar – nor I. 'Pale hands pink-tipped, like lotus buds that float on those blue waters where we used to dwell.' I cried myself to sleep because she wasn't with me, because she was somewhere else, in another room; yet the idea of going to bed with her, which never crossed my mind as a desire, would have been sacrilege. I didn't know that I wanted to. The serpent rampant, even at her presence in the same room, seemed to me to have nothing to do with the situation, an outrage that made me furious with my gross body, and to punish it I refused myself the relief that was more urgently necessary than ever before.

Yet thinking of it afterwards, back in the little circle of our own household, I found a comparison that I have never to this day seen expressed; the longings that I had experienced, the strange, inseparable blend of pain and delight, seemed in fact the exact emotional counterpart of the agonized ecstasies my body could provide. By that realization I glimpsed that these were two separate manifestations of the same thing, and I saw momentarily what unbelievable happiness might lie in their conjunction. Some time, far away in the future; not this year, not next year; sometime, but not never.

14

THE END OF EXILE

IN THE WINTER after my illness, when I was allowed up and even to go for short walks out of doors, I was moved a mile from Northfield to a little house adjoining the Apostolic Chapel. This house was lent to my mother by a neighbour, because it had a southern exposure and could benefit by whatever sunshine an English winter could provide. The bedrooms at Northfield faced west, and faced, too, into high yew hedges. To me any move was a move towards freedom, a move, implicitly, towards Elrig, and I took up residence at Cook's Place with a sudden rebirth of hope in the future.

The *ménage* consisted of my mother, my sister Christian and her ageing and evil-smelling Yorkshire terrier Carlo; myself, with my brash yellow-eyed spaniel in a kennel in the garden, and a prissy middle-aged daily tutor whose name was Mr Turner but whom my sister with an unerring eye for apposite nicknames had rechristened The Turnip.

That winter was like a battle. Like all battles it had its ups and downs, its sorties and retreats; but like an archetypal battle it was all-absorbing to me, the contestant, and I was aware of the struggle during every waking hour. I was utterly determined that no concession granted to me should be withdrawn; I would have hidden or disguised any symptom of illness that was in my power to camouflage rather than run the faintest risk of being put back to bed. This became an obsession with me, equalled only by what had now become the real obsession with sex usual in most people of my age. (I didn't know that it was usual; this was nineteen years before the Kinsey Report.) I had stopped fighting with that, the only aspect of my body's strength; what I fought now was its appalling, literal weakness in all other spheres. In this I think

I must have applied more determination than I had ever given to anything in my life.

I can remember every incident, and the infinite subterfuge I employed to cover what I saw as the tracks of a wounded animal. The first was after a fall of snow a few days before Christmas. There was a bright sun and a sharp frost, and before breakfast I set off across the lawn to cover the twenty yards to my dog's kennel. I had covered perhaps half the distance before my head seemed to become detached from my body. I knew that my limbs were struggling away somewhere down below, but my head was ten or twenty feet above the ground, and it was sightless; there was nothing before my eyes but infinite shifting seas of red. I lost all sense of direction; my legs staggered on without any orientation to my goal, and after a few seconds my hip hit something hard and I came to a stop. My hands, so far below my blind giraffe head, explored and found a fence post; I held on to the wire and followed it until my legs bumped into the kennel. It was a big kennel; still blind, I managed to drop down on all fours and creep into it beside the dog, where I lost consciousness. I came round with the dog licking my face. After a moment or two of rallying myself I peered out of the kennel door. No one had noticed anything, but the footprints in the snow showed disastrously, and couldn't possibly be explained away. I crawled out and got to my feet and found I felt much as usual, so I took the dog off his chain and as he ran round the lawn I set about covering the whole snow surface with my footprints and his, so that the wavering zigzag track would be lost among a hundred others.

The next time I was playing golf with my sister at Bramley golf course five miles away. After the first few holes I began to experience waves of dizziness in which I had to lean on a golf-club to prevent myself falling. It took all the will-power I had to disguise this from my sister, and I started to make weak jokes so that she would think I was in high spirits. But I knew that collapse was very near, and the only thing for it was somehow to get out of sight. I did this by slicing my ball into a dense clump of gorse bushes, giving my sister the hole, and saying I would meet her on the next tee after I had found my ball. When I was well in among the gorse bushes I lay down and fainted. As in the dog-kennel I felt almost normal when I regained consciousness, but I knew I couldn't risk going on playing. I had two spare balls in the pocket of my golf-bag, and I knew my sister had none. I buried these two spares deep in the thicket, peered out to see that my sister was only now arriving on the tee, and called to her that I couldn't find the ball, that I had no more, and so we would have to go home. I got away with it, as I did many other occasions, because of my bitter determination not to be reduced again to the captivity of bed. When I had 'flu or a feverish cold I would try, when my mother took my temperature, to get her out of the room for long enough to shake the mercury down to normal, and once I even palmed a second thermometer, pre-set at normal, and gave her back this instead of the one that I knew would show a fever. All this was extremely foolish, but it seemed to me absolutely necessary as a step to freedom and manhood and return to Elrig.

But Elrig was still far off, and during the whole of that year we never went there, for my mother felt that it was too far from specialized medical help. We moved back to Northfield in the spring, and I attended a cramming establishment in Goldalming, as a day pupil, and during the lessons I spent much of my time dreaming of Elrig as I had done at Stowe.

The year was brightened for me by possession of the first indoor dog that I had ever been allowed to own. Judy was a little Red Cocker Spaniel bitch, and she was just two months old when she came. She never grew to be more than about half the size of an ordinary cocker; from the show-bench point of view she was hardly a cocker at all, for she belonged to the old race before the fashion for narrow brainless skulls and drooping ears attached somewhere halfway down the neck. She had a broad skull, ears fixed on where they belong and which she would fan forward like an elephant's when she was interested; soulful brown eyes, and more brain than any dog I have ever known. She became inseparable from me, and I found that I could teach her anything, from parlour tricks such as whispering or shouting when asked, to the complicated gundog work for which spaniels were originally bred. She was hardly ever out of my sight during the five years that she lived.

I learned to drive my mother's Rover on the long drive of Albury Park, so that on my seventeenth birthday I became my mother's chauffeur, and she never employed one again. We

'ears.. which she would fan forwards, like an elephant's when she was interested.'

started on a long tour of all her scattered girlhood friends in distant castles and country mansions, in which I was dismayed to find that I was as tongue-tied and shy as I had been at Alnwick two years earlier; but during that year I gradually learned, if not how to make conversation, at least to avoid social blunders born of ignorance. I learned scales of tipping and what was the least that one could give to a butler; and all the little rituals that together composed the password of the tribe, and as fast as I learned the totems and taboos I conformed fanatically. Conformity was what I craved as never before, for in the tribal sense I was homeless; the tribe of the family seemed to have disbanded, the tribe of school was over, and I was conscious of the need to be adopted by another tribe quickly. I rarely met anyone of my own age in the great houses we visited, but the adults were generally kind, and the men warmed to me when they discovered my passion for, and knowledge of, shooting. When they praised my skill and told me that I would assuredly be as fine a shot as my father or my Uncle Willie, I was swept into the Game Book Group on the wings of their flattery.

After this Grand Tour, the next six months or so of my convalescence I spent moving about with my mother between supposedly health-giving spots on the south coast of England. Of these I remember best a beautiful little farmhouse near Kingsbridge, Devon, in which we were paying guests, and I remember it because of an exceedingly brief but equally memorable appearance of my brother Eustace. It was an exquisite little Queen Anne house that had been preserved without blemish or modernization, a 'bijou' affair of mellowed red brick and white wood, with a perfect pillared porch, and it stood upon a green lawn so immaculate that the whole had an air almost of artificiality.

Eustace, aged eighteen and just entered Sandhurst, visited us for one night. He arrived in the evening in an open Talbot 14/40, and seeing that the gravel space in front of the porch was too small for the car to turn easily, he reversed on to the green lawn – quite a long way on to it. There had been heavy showers and the ground was soft; when he tried to regain the gravel his rear wheels dug in deeply; and the more, in his inexperience, he revved the engine in low gear the deeper they dug. By the time the farmer was called, the lawn was in quite a mess. The farmer said little, and brought horses. Their direct pull would not move the car, and only added one-ton hoof-prints to the defaced surface, so either the farmer or Eustace suggested passing a rope round one of the pillars of the beautiful porch and thus gaining purchase. The horses strained, Eustace revved his engine to help them. Suddenly there was a sound of grinding and crackling and down came the pillar, and with it most of the porch.

The magnitude of damage caused during that first hour was so monstrous that both Eustace and I began to get the giggles with which our family had always been cursed. My mother, distracted by the whole appalling exhibition, became exceedingly angry, and the atmosphere during the evening was like that of all too many family reunions the world over.

Somehow the car was finally restored to the gravel, in correct alignment for departure the following morning, and we all went to bed. As I have said, the house had never been modernized, and there was no electric light. Eustace went upstairs carrying a candle, to a room that the farmer had vacated for him, the farmer having moved for the night to a downstairs room directly below. Just as there was no electricity, so there was no running water in the bedrooms, and the wash-hand stands were equipped with huge china basins and china water-jugs that can have held little less than three gallons.

Eustace's potential for destruction was far from exhausted. His candle blew out in the draught as he opened his bedroom door, and he blundered straight into the wash-hand stand. There was a really surprisingly large crash as the jug and basin hit the floor and broke into fragments. Water began to pour through the ceiling on to the farmer's bed below.

At this point Eustace decided that it would be wise to leave before the necessity for further explanations could arise. Knowing that farmers rise early, he rose earlier still, while we were all asleep, and in the very first light of dawn he tip-toed downstairs and out through the ruined porch to his car. The drive was short and steep to a narrow Devonshire lane running at right angles, where two ornamental white gateposts, in keeping with the rest of the house and garden, flanked the entrance. He turned left into the lane, but he turned too sharply; the rear end of the car brought the gatepost down. He did not return; in fact he did not even stop – realizing that the situation was by now wholly irremediable he sped northwards in the growing light.

His visit had lasted ten hours; the damage amounted, if I remember rightly, to £140.

Winter in Bournemouth, and a daily tutor who had been my brother Eustace's in France; a small, elderly Englishman with twirled white moustaches, who had been domiciled for the greater part of his life in Tours. I had enough adolescent aggression to resent, without sympathy, his halitosis and his preciosity, his monologues on food and wine; it was at this point that I adopted what Kingsley Amis has described as 'Not the wondering gaze of childhood but the cold, angry stare of the adolescent'. I saw everyone I met through this cold angry stare; nobody pleased me. I met no one, literally no one, of my own age, and the repository of all my yearning affection became the little Cocker Spaniel bitch Judy. I felt that we understood each other and loved each other, and when I could take her for walks alone in the deep Scottish-seeming heather glades and pine woods of Ringwood Forest, so lonely and so utterly unspoilt, I was as near to happiness as my state of mutiny would allow.

I had no other confidant. During all that winter in Bournemouth I knew nobody but my mother and my tutor. When he would tell a story about food, lasting half an hour, I gave him the cold angry stare and avoided my mother's glance. I still remember some of those food stories. Eels, he said, wiping his well-tended but yellow-stained white moustache, could be the best food in the world, but this he had not discovered until he had been travelling alone in such and such a province of France a few years before. There was little else on the menu but omelettes, and having eaten one of these he proceeded to his great discovery. ' "D'accord," I said to the patron. "You may serve me with eels – which are not my favourite food – but don't let the sauce be too rich." I said this because the sauces of that province, which are delicious, are sometimes dyspeptic, and I have to be careful. I am a gourmet, but my palate has proved more immortal than my digestion. So I said this, "Don't let the sauce be too rich." And do you know what the *patron* replied? He said: "Monsieur, there will be no sauce." And I said in great astonishment: "What, no sauce?" And he said: "No, Monsieur, no sauce. The eel has been marinated for five days in a marinade which is *ours*, Monsieur, and no one else's, and then baked in black butter and sour cream." So I said I would try it, and I asked him what wine he would give me to drink with the eel, and he said: "A wine from my own vineyard, Monsieur." Now I do not care for the wines of that district – that is a question of *goût*, for they are sound wines, you understand – but he asked me to trust him and try, and do you know that eel and that half-bottle of deliciously dry white wine were all that even I could have asked? After them I smoked an Havana of my own, of course, and though the cognac was inferior I was not by that time in a critical mood.' This kind of monologue from the poor gentle old gourmet produced in me a silent fury that was part of my general rebellion.

This was winter in Bournemouth, winter in a boarding-house with the black fabric Rover parked in front of the (just) detached house in a suburban street. The street was dead. Though I never lost sight of my target – Elrig and total emancipation – each day I had more immediate and urgent goals. I wanted either to take the car and walk alone with Judy in the wildness of Ringwood Forest, or to go down into the town, to the main streets and the esplanade, where I could watch a throng of human beings and fantasy myself into some deep romantic relationship with any face that caught my fancy. Only rarely did I get the chance to make this last kind of excursion, and when I did I was confused. One woman and one man tried to pick me up, and in each case I fled. I never rationalized this behaviour; I wanted some physical relationship so desperately and so terribly that it seemed to me that the need must destroy me. I became rude and sullen. Possibly my tutor knew enough of youth to armour himself, but my mother had no such continuing pattern behind her; as the last of her children with whom she retained a womb relationship, my kicking must have been real pain. We no longer understood each other, so each of us stumbled on new, random ways of wounding without knowing it. It was the very worst period of my adolescent life; hurting and being hurt, fighting for a degree of freedom that I could not have used had I suddenly been granted it. How could my mother have understood this turmoil, essentially sexual, that broke a long pattern of dependence and good manners. I hated everything that confined me, and I hated it with a sharp, edged resentment.

When at last I knew we were going back to Elrig in the spring I assessed cold-bloodedly the cards in my hand. I had disguised my fainting-fits and dizziness, and I had surrendered only once, in panic, when for the second time I saw purple spots on my ankles, and in a nightmare of fear I sought reassurance. (Until I was eighteen those dreaded stigmata recurred every time that I reached a certain stage of physical exhaustion.) Now I was apparently healthy, and I had taken my School Certificate; I needed somehow to make good the past, to bring it together into my own hands. Long ago when I was in the nursing-home John Kent had asked me to stay with him in Cheshire; now I could assert my survival by asking him to stay at Elrig. I wrote to him, and for a few days after that his acceptance or refusal became the most important thing in my life.

Envelopes, like smells, are remembered things. I remember his, the very blue ink, the handwriting beginning to be formed, the stamp askew. The letter of acceptance was like a huge cumulus cloud constantly changing shape; and thus full of infinite possibility. He would be my own guest and my first guest, not my mother's nor my brother's nor the guest of circumstance, but mine, and he would unite the departed world of Stowe with the future world of Elrig.

John and I explored the kingdom from which I had been exiled for so long, the high, wind-whining moorlands of rock and heather, the far hill and sea horizons; and in his company I consolidated a long-lost position. We went to look for an eagle's nest in the Galloway Hills, and as we scrambled up the rain-gleaming rock and scree I asked, because this was important, 'John, what do you ordinarily do in the holidays?' He said: 'Well, nothing as good as this,' and suddenly the rock and the rain and all the gigantic windswept kingdom of Galloway seemed mine to live in, all exile over.

A SELECTION OF
POPULAR READING IN PAN

THE DEATH OF A PRESIDENT 12/6

William Manchester

'Magnificent . . . high definition reporting of the most meticulous and precise standard, blended with the right amount of emotion . . . An epic with a cast of thousands, and a definitive piece of research . . . William Manchester has produced a book the like of which has not been written before.' Daily Express

'Totally compulsive reading . . . I recommend this book to students—not of history, but of the fascinating, unpredictable, emotional and sentimental behaviour of human beings at a moment of unimaginable crisis and horror.' Sunday Mirror

'But murder is murder, and it is vile and it is ghastly, and you cannot avoid it. You can't dodge it. It isn't easy to write, but you've got to do it if you are going to tell the truth.' William Manchester, BBC 'World of Books'

'In the sheer telling of a story he succeeds brilliantly. The tension is unbearable even though the plot is no mystery . . .' Economist

'A masterly piece of overall planning . . . a grand undertaking.' Sunday Times